THE UPLANDS
A Great Camp
in the Adirondacks

THE
UPLANDS
A Great Camp
in the Adirondacks

A Memoir & Cookbook

Phebe Thorne

Second edition

Edited and produced by Colleen Daly
First Edition Design by Faith Hague
Second Edition Design & Production by Richard Whittington

www.phebebooks.com

Names: Thorne, Phebe, author. | Harris, Ralph, (Illustrator), illustrator.
Title: The Uplands : a great camp in the Adirondacks : a memoir & cookbook / Phebe Thorne ; [illustrations by Ralph Harris].
Description: Second edition. | Ketchum, ID : [Phebe Thorne], [2021] | Previously published as: Camp cooking in the Adirondacks. | Includes index.
Identifiers: ISBN 9780578876139 (hardcover) | LCCN 2021908594
Subjects: LCSH: Thorne, Phebe--Family. | Keene Valley (N.Y.)--Biography. | Camps--New York (State)--Adirondack Mountains. | Outdoor cooking. | Entertaining. | LCGFT: Cookbooks. | Autobiographies.
Classification: LCC F127.E8 T46 2021 | DDC 974.753092--dc2

Printed in Canada by Friesens
10 9 8 7 6 5 4 3 2 1

PHOTO & PRINTS CREDITS

Cover, pages 2, 25, 26, 29, 31, 65, 66, 87, 115, 136, 139, 157, 218, 225: by Gary Hall, GaryHallPhoto.com
p. 6: by Mary Beth Flower
p. 42: by Helaine Balsam
p. 49: by Naj Wikoff
p. 57: by Lisa Ryan-Boyle
p. 63: by Richard Whittington
p. 120: by Colleen Daly
p. 131: by Richard Whittington
p. 146: by Sarah Luke
p. 227: by Richard Whittington
Back cover (The Uplands): by Naj Wikoff

Chapter openers courtesy of the Adirondack Experience Collection:
p. 64: "Mount Haystack. From Upper Ausable Inlet," by Verplanck Colvin, printed by Weed, Parsons and Co., 1880.
p. 74: "Camping Out. 'Some of the Right Sort,'" by Louis Maurer, engraved by Currier & Ives, 1856.
p. 104: "In the Adirondacks – Camping in the Upper Ausable," by Homer Dodge Martin, engraved by John Parker Davis, 1870.
p. 122: "Trapping in the Adirondacks," by Winslow Homer, engraved by John Parker Davis, 1870.
p. 132: "The Hunter's Shanty. In the Adirondacks," engraved by Currier & Ives, 1861.
p. 150: "Christmas in Camp – Tying Up the Pudding," by Arthur Burdett Frost I, woodblock on paper, 1885.
p. 196: "The Centennial – The Hunter's Camp," by Theodore Davis Russell, 1876.
p. 210: "Camping Out in the Adirondack Mountains," by Winslow Homer, engraved by W.H. Lagarde, 1874.
p. 222: "Her First Muskallonge," by Frederic Remington, 1888.

Other images from the Adirondack Experience Collection:
p. 41: "View From the Stern Seat," Charlie Blanchard – a guide from Blue Mountain Lake, by Seneca Ray Stoddard, 1888.
p. 67: "An Amateur Cook," Harper & Brothers, 1891.

Illustrations by Ralph Harris (except pages 19, 55, 67 & 69)

This book is dedicated to my husband, Neil Ryan,
who helped me restore and run the Uplands for the last 10 years,
and who encouraged me to tell the stories
about the house and its occupants.

Special Thanks

Helena Thorne Marrin Grant

My daughter grew up at The Uplands. For her entire life she has spent her summers and many holidays and weekends in Keene Valley. I am so grateful for her companionship and her passion for the Adirondacks and her family history.

Naj Wikoff and I supported each other's non-profits for many years, and he managed three garage sales at the Uplands! I thank him now for his beautiful 2020 photo of The Uplands, and the photo – in "The Guestbooks" essay – of his painting of the Owl on our signpost.

In order to protect The Uplands, which our family has loved for almost 100 years, I chose **Jenny Clark**. Having already restored an old carriage house in Connecticut, she wanted to restore and modernize The Uplands to its proper glory, and she did a wonderful job!

Richard Longstreth and I were on two boards together for many years: Fort Ticonderoga and AARCH. The Fort has many structures in need of restoration, but especially the Pavilion, which was recently restored – with the help of many – and it opens to the public just as this book is being published.

AARCH works to save and restore historic structures all over the Adirondacks. It was AARCH and Richard who encouraged me to apply to the National Register of Historic Places to include The Uplands on the Register.

Acknowledgments

I would like to acknowledge my editor, Colleen Daly, whom I met in Sun Valley while she was Executive Director of the Community Library. She visited me at The Uplands and encouraged me to write about the life of the house. She pushed, she encouraged, she inspired, and she kept me on task. She made this book possible.

I would also like to acknowledge Executive Director Aurora McCaffrey at the Essex County Historical Society, Registrar Hanna Person at the Adirondack Experience, and Stuart Lilie, Vice President of Public History at Fort Ticonderoga – all of whom answered questions about important details.

Contents

Part I: The UPLANDS A Memoir

It is time to tell the story of the house called The Uplands, and the stories of the people who lived there. It's also time to bring out the second edition of *Camp Cooking in the Adirondacks, Easy Entertaining at The Uplands*, which was published in 2006 while I was living in both the Adirondacks and in Sun Valley, Idaho. The title of this edition is *The Uplands: A Great Camp in the Adirondacks, A Memoir & Cookbook*.

The original *Camp Cooking* is full of recipes for yummy meals that are simple to prepare after a morning or a day of hiking, canoeing, skiing, or otherwise adventuring in the great outdoors – which is what life in the Adirondacks and life in Sun Valley offers up. Of course, in this version I couldn't resist including some of my new favorite recipes.

This second edition will be also be a memoir of The Uplands. There are lots of stories – some are historical, some are funny, some are sad. But, that is just life! The life of the house is the life of those who lived in it, and those who visited it.

Mom pumping water for me

The Life of the House & the People Who Lived There

My Name is Phebe

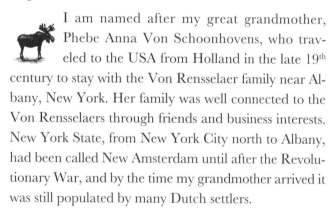 I am named after my great grandmother, Phebe Anna Von Schoonhovens, who traveled to the USA from Holland in the late 19th century to stay with the Von Rensselaer family near Albany, New York. Her family was well connected to the Von Rensselaers through friends and business interests. New York State, from New York City north to Albany, had been called New Amsterdam until after the Revolutionary War, and by the time my grandmother arrived it was still populated by many Dutch settlers.

Phebe arrived at her host's home, a large mansion on a hill overlooking the Hudson River, which was the main north-south highway for passengers and freight in that part of the world. The room she stayed in was on the second floor and had a balcony over the front door, which meant she could see who was arriving to meet her. Her hosts had plans to introduce her to all the fine young men they knew. There were dances and lunches and dinners and overnight guests if they had travelled far.

Phebe was very attractive, with long cream-colored hair, a long neck, a small head, and a slim figure. She was a gifted pianist and entertained family and visitors each night after dinner.

Once they had introduced her to all the local boys, the Von Rensselaers expanded their list of appropriate young men to include those living in Millbrook, New York, where the Thornes had a house. Having already proved himself to be successful in business and farming, Samuel Thorne was probably about 25 years old in 1870. The distance between Millbrook and Rensselaer is approximately 35 miles, so young Mr. Thorne was invited to stay for three days.

Phebe was on her balcony watching as Sam drove up in a small road cart drawn by a high-stepping hackney. They say she swooned at first sight.

It was a quick and successful courtship. They married six months after being introduced. Soon they moved to New York City, where the Thornes had a tanning business, and where they had started a bank. Their first child was a son, my grandfather, also named Samuel.

My granddad told me they lived in a townhouse on Fifth Avenue where the Pierre Hotel now sits, not far from the southern edge of Central Park. Music was an important part of family life. As she had done before she married, Phebe entertained guests with a piano concert each evening after dinner. The family went to Carnegie Hall concerts and were supportive of and friendly with the conductor and musicians. This enthusiasm would eventually be realized as a summer retreat in the Adirondacks, built by my granddad for musicians who could not afford a summer vacation away from the hot city.

Granddad said that when he was a boy he saw his parents only once a day, for a meeting in the afternoon after school in the very large living room. His father would ask him how he was doing in his classes, and Granddad would answer that he was doing just fine. The visits were short, without hugs or kisses, which he received only from his nanny.

After graduating from Yale in 1896 and then law school in 1899, Granddad married Ethel Mary Cheney in 1901. Their first-born was a son, yet another Samuel. The second child was my father, Lewis. Altogether my father's parents had seven children – six sons and a daughter.

My grandmother died of congestive heart failure in 1937, and the following year my father married Helen Preston Ellis, my mother. Her childhood had been filled with many hugs and kisses, and also music. When she first met my grandfather she gave him a kiss on the cheek and a hug. He fell in love with her that very moment and the two of them were quite close for the rest of their lives.

Helen Preston Ellis

My mother was born in 1913 in Waban, Massachusetts, a small town one hour west of Boston. She was the second child of four. Her mother was an accomplished pianist and opera singer who spent her days practicing for private salon concerts. Because music was such an important part of her childhood, Helen grew to love the piano and became a talented pianist herself, but she dreaded the scales and warm-ups for opera.

My mother's father, Reuben Morris Ellis, worked for a tobacco company buying tobacco all over the world. He would become the first president of Philip

Morris; his signature was scrawled across the cigarette pack. His work travels kept him away from home during most of my mother's childhood, but when he was with his family it was always magical. He told stories of faraway places, interesting people, and different customs. He was affectionate and fun. He died of a heart attack when my mother was 18.

My mother had been accepted into the London Conservatory of Music, but she wanted to be a nurse and not a concert pianist. One day she sneaked off and took the train from Boston to New York, where she enrolled in the Presbyterian Hospital School of Nursing, now called Columbia School of Nursing. That is where she met my father.

Handsome and charming, Lewis Thorne was a medical intern at Columbia University Medical Center in the fall of 1936, having graduated from Yale University in 1931, and then Yale Medical School in June 1936.

Mom was starting her second year of nursing school at Columbia in 1936. They fell madly in love and he proposed. He had been accepted at John Hopkins Hospital for his three-year residency, so they would live in Baltimore. Mom had to quit nursing because back then you were not allowed to be married *and* be a nursing student!

The wedding took place on August 21, 1937, and after their honeymoon they went off to Baltimore. Then in 1941 they moved to New Haven, where Dad worked at Yale Student Health as a doctor for the students at Yale. I was born in February of 1941. My name: Phebe Ellis Thorne. At the time there were six Phebe Thornes in the family, most of them distant cousins, and all of them a generation older.

Helen Preston Ellis and Lewis Thorne

That December, after the bombing of Pearl Harbor, the United States entered World War II. My father enlisted in early 1942, but before joining the troops he spent a year at Emory University as Major Dr. Lewis Thorne. We moved to Atlanta for his residency, which focused on war-type injuries and on mental stresses related to war.

The U.S. Army was advertising for recruits who could ski and camp out in the winter. My father, passionate about mountaineering since he was young, had spent two years after graduating from Yale and before starting medical school climbing the highest peaks in China and Nepal with his pals. He had tried to climb Everest, but his party had been forced to turn back when two of them froze their toes, which had to be amputated.

Dad had learned how to ski in Switzerland and Austria. He was just the sort of recruit they were looking for in the Tenth Mountain Division of the U.S Army. He called his friends from the Dartmouth Outing Club, and other friends who had climbed and skied with him. They all signed up for this great adventure.

In the fall of 1943, our family moved to Colorado. I remember the trip west in the Green Hornet, a convertible Buick that had a small hammock you could string up in the back to hold the top when it was down. My mom and I lived in a small cabin while Dad trained with the Tenth on what is now Aspen Mountain and was then called Ajax. This was a full three years before the ski resort opened.

Our cabin, surrounded by miles of fencing to keep cattle in, was located 15 miles from the town of Aspen, which was a long trip on a snowy road. This meant we could only go to town once a week to shop for food (everything was rationed anyway).

The cabin was heated by a fireplace in the main room and a wood-burning stove in the kitchen, both of which were kept going all the time. They had died out once, early in our stay, and after that Mom learned the art of banking the fires and using a big log to keep us warm through the night. The only water came from a hand pump on the kitchen counter. Once a week, Mom heated a big bucket of water on the stove and I had a bath in a tin tub in front of the fire. I remember that as a very special treat. I had a little pony to ride, even though I was only two. I have loved horses ever since.

Once Dad finished his training and left for the Dolomites, in the northern Italian Alps between Switzerland and Austria, Mom and I returned to Atlanta. Dad came home twice on leave, once in 1944, when I was three. That August my little sister, Cynthia (Cindy) Neale Thorne, was born. Neale was the name of Dad's brother, James Neale, who had joined the RAF before the U.S. went to war. A fighter pilot, he was shot down over Belgium during the Battle of the Bulge soon after Cindy was born.

When the war ended, Dad – now Lieutenant Colonel Thorne – came home after finishing his tour of duty, and we packed up again to head back to New Haven, where he would start his career. It was 1946 and he had been promised a position at Yale studying dream analysis and practicing medicine. Once again we drove in the Green Hornet packed full of our belongings. On the way to Connecticut, my sister and I were dropped off in Rye, New York, to live with Granddad until Mom and Dad could find a home for all of us. There was a severe housing shortage after the war, as no new houses had been built during those years.

It seemed forever before Mom and Dad came back to get us. It was probably a few weeks.

Our first house was at 11 Summit Road, a small colonial in a convenient location. I could walk to kindergarten at the public school a mile away, and Dad could take the bus into the Medical Center. Mom drove the Green Hornet.

My mother and sister and I had spent the last few years in the South where people greeted each other by saying, "Hey, y'all!" But when my new teacher heard me say such a thing she scowled and told me, "Hay is for horses. Go stand in the hall until you learn how to say hello." It took a few times in the hall for me to learn to talk like a polite Yankee.

We moved to 25 Old Orchard Road when I was eight. The house had been built in an old apple orchard, and there were at least 20 apple trees in our yard. Dad and I built a tree house in one of them. That first fall, and for many falls after that, our home was transformed into a mad house when the apples were ready. I helped harvest the apples, which Mom cooked up into apple sauce, and apple brown betty, and apple butter, and apple pies to freeze. Eventually we would haul all the apples we hadn't processed to the cider mill and bring home gallons of cider.

On October 8, 1950, Mom came home from an operation. We were so happy to see her! After feeding me and Cindy early, my parents kissed us goodnight so they could have a quiet dinner in front of the living-room fire. I had almost fallen asleep when I heard a loud POP – POP – POP sound.

I flew downstairs and saw Mom on the foyer floor with blood oozing out of her head. She said, "Get the Gambles!" I ran across the street, jumped over the Gambles' picket fence, and burst through the door and into their house screaming, "Mom is lying on the floor all bloody!"

Although Mom had been shot through the head, she was awake when they took her to the hospital, and she was able to identify the shooter. During the operation the doctors stitched up what they could. The bullet had entered next to her right eye and passed through her head, nipping the auditory nerve and facial nerve and exiting behind her left ear. It was amazing that she lost only the feeling on the left side of her face, and the hearing in her left ear.

Mom later said that Dad had stood up when a man entered the living room with a gun pointed at them. Everything happened so fast. The man fired and hit Dad in the shoulder. Dad told Mom to leave, but the man fired again, and that shot went through Dad's heart, so he fell over. Then Mom attacked the man, trying to gouge his eyes out with her lovely, long, red nails. She remembered seeing the gun pointed at her head, and she heard the shot.

Trent Lyon had been a patient of Dad's. But when it became clear he was a danger to himself and others, Dad and six other psychiatrists went to court and had him committed to a secure mental institution in Middletown, Connecticut. Trent had escaped, gone to a hardware store, bought a gun, looked up Dr. Lewis Thorne in the phone book, and walked into our house.

He escaped four more times, always intent on finding and killing Mom. The authorities were always alerted, and caught him before he got to her, but he came close more than once. He died shortly before Mom did, so she lived with this threat for 50 years.

They didn't tell Mom that Dad was dead because they thought she would give up trying to live. Cindy went to stay with the Loesers, across the street, and I went to my Aunt Vera and Uncle Sam in Old Lyme. Cindy and I were not told about the funeral. They thought it would be too upsetting.

But how could it be other than upsetting to know your Father is dead and your Mother gravely injured? How wrong to deny a child the comfort of the community embrace and mutual mourning. It didn't really hit me that I had missed all of that until Uncle Bob was about to walk me down the aisle to marry Billy, and I burst into tears. I sobbed and sobbed that Daddy wasn't there to walk with me.

And then, when Baby Katherine was dying, I finally went to a psychologist to work things out. I could love so intensely, but it could all be gone so quickly.

Ethel Mary Cheney Was My Paternal Grandmother

She was born a Lee and became a Cheney in the first year of her life. Her mother, Mary Katherine Molette – from a wealthy, Southern family – had shocked her French Huguenot parents by falling in love with and marrying a damn Yankee! He was Charles Tennant Lee from Boston. They married in Europe, and once back home, Charles worked well on the Molette plantation properties. He and Mary Katherine had a happy marriage with three children: Virginia, Frances, and Charles Tennant, Jr. Then Mary Eliza was born on March 9, 1878.

Five days later, Mary Eliza Lee's mother died, having been infected in the hospital with scarlet fever by the midwife who had attended her. Her devastated father chose to return to the family house in Boston where he would live with his mother and sister, 23-year-old Frances, who would help him raise the three young children. But what about the newborn?

A close friend of the Lee family, Mrs. Arthur (Emeline Lewis) Cheney, the godmother of daughter Frances, desperately wanted a child. It was love at first sight when she met and started taking care of baby Mary Eliza. Adoption proceedings were finalized in October of 1878, less than two weeks after Arthur Cheney suddenly fell ill and died. Emeline had lost her husband but gained a daughter.

In spite of the tragedies, Mary Eliza Lee, now Ethel Mary Cheney, became one of dozens of loving cousins living in four great mansions on a hill in Manchester, Connecticut, looking down at the Farmington River. Ethel and her cousins studied and played together, going from house to house as freely as if it were one tight campus, which it actually was since the entire neighborhood had been created by Ethel's grandparents as the headquarters of the Cheney silk empire.

Silk was ever more fashionable in the U.S. as people had become wealthier during the Industrial Era. Women wanted silk dresses and blouses. Men wanted silk ties and vests. Ethel's grandfather, Ward Cheney, and his brothers had started their silk business in the 1830s by cultivating mulberry trees and raising silkworms on an industrial scale. Then in 1840 the mulberry market crashed because of overplanting and a mulberry blight.

The Cheney brothers, ahead of the curve, had already shifted their focus from trying to grow their own silkworms to importing the cocoons from Japan, and then to importing bales of raw silk from China, Japan, and Italy to Manchester. They produced the finest silk: brocades and *peau de soie* and other satin and silks so fine and sheer that some of it was used for ladies' stockings.

They hired skilled operators from Europe and developed innovative silk-production methods and spinning technologies. Expanding slowly, they built more mills, and eventually had almost 5,000 employees. Workers were from all different backgrounds and races; what

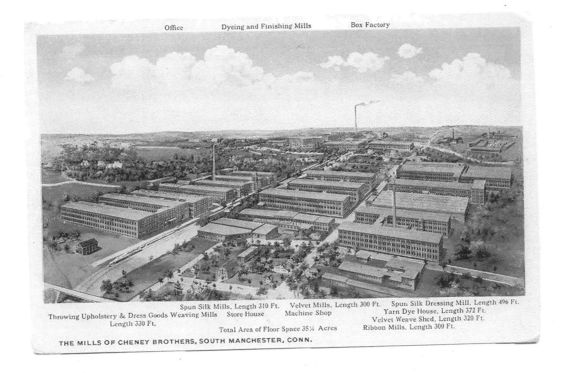

Office   Dyeing and Finishing Mills   Box Factory

Spun Silk Mills, Length 310 Ft.   Velvet Mills, Length 300 Ft.   Spun Silk Dressing Mill, Length 496 Ft.
Throwing Upholstery & Dress Goods Weaving Mills   Store House   Machine Shop   Yarn Dye House, Length 372 Ft.
Length 330 Ft.   Velvet Weave Shed, Length 320 Ft.
Total Area of Floor Space 35¼ Acres   Ribbon Mills, Length 300 Ft.

THE MILLS OF CHENEY BROTHERS, SOUTH MANCHESTER, CONN.

mattered was a good work effort and some dexterity. To encourage the workers, the Cheneys offered housing and good wages. Every house was different, but each had at least two bedrooms, a kitchen, and a parlor, as well as an outhouse. No doubt inspired by trips to Japan, the Cheneys built communal bathing houses with showers and hot pools for all employees and their families to use – with separate buildings for men and for women.

For meetings and entertainment and large communal dinners, the brothers built Cheney Hall soon after the end of the Civil War. This was the true heart of the community. A nearby church was the soul. The large park-like area known as the Great Lawn in front of the mansions was open to the public, who came to pick dandelions, find worms for fish-bait, and in winter to ski, sled, and toboggan. Today this entire site is a 175-acre historic district in downtown Manchester.

In the summer, the entire Cheney clan would go to their camp, Sunset Hill, in the Adirondacks, near a small town called Keene Valley. They hiked the mountains and swam in the cold pools of the Ausable and Bouquet rivers. There was no electricity, but at night they sat by the fire in the living room, and one person would read aloud to the whole family. They went to bed early, slept well after a day outdoors, and awoke as the sun came up, eager for more hiking, swimming, boating, and picnicking in the mountains.

Ethel grew to be a bright and charming young lady. I don't know how she met Samuel Thorne, who grew up in New York City, but they were married in 1901, two years after Samuel graduated from Harvard Law School. So it was Ethel who took Samuel to Keene Valley for the first time. He fell in love with the beautiful mountain environment, and they returned every summer.

Over the summers, as their family grew to seven children (six boys and one girl!) by 1916, Ethel and Samuel rented the Silver Birches Cottage at the Ausable Club. In 1922 they bought their own place, from the Allings, Ausable Club members they knew. And that is how The Uplands came into the Thorne family.

Built in 1909, The Uplands was then a nine-bedroom "camp" meant for summer use. The rooms and porches were large and the property included 50 acres, a pond, an ice house, a laundry house, and a garage for three cars – with a small apartment for the chauffeur. In 1925 they added the South House, which was built off the kitchen (at the south end of the main house) for the staff. The South House had five bedrooms and two bathrooms, was "winterized," and had a coal-burning boiler in the basement for heat.

Granddad, by then in his late 40s, had the foresight to envision visiting The Uplands during hunting season, and hiking along the trails ablaze with fall colors. I do not think he ever imagined anyone would want to visit in the long, frozen winters to ski!

But eventually the laundry house became the kitchen and dining room during the winters, and the next three generations of Thornes and their guests enjoyed many weekends hunting in the fall and skiing in the winter.

The Farm: Uplands Meadows, Inc.

I'm not sure when Granddad bought the farm, but I suspect it was about 1938 or 1939, after Grandmother had died and all the boys and Aunt Em had graduated from college. The farm, named Upland Meadows, Inc., was a dairy farm that produced all the milk for the Ausable Valley from St. Huberts – where the club is – to Au Sable Forks. The barns and farmer's house were made from field stones turned up during the clearing and plowing of the land for growing hay to feed the Guernseys during winter.

The picturesque farm sits in a basin rimmed on all sides by mountains and surrounded by fields of hay and meadows of grazing cows. To reach it you drive up the long four-mile hill on Stiles Brook Road between Keene and Upper Jay. When you crest the hill and turn slightly left, there it is, spread out below.

A stay at The Uplands always included a trip to the farm for a visit to the cows and to watch the milking in the late afternoon. We were allowed to pet the two Belgian horses who pulled the wagon for haying in the summer and the sleigh for sugaring in the spring. We usually came home with a kitten or two.

While we visited once a year, Granddad went EVERY day. He was a lawyer, but if you asked him what he did he would say, "I am a farmer in upstate New York." Even on rainy days he went there to fix something or help somebody or pull old rusty nails out of boards so they could be reused for fencing.

Our milk at The Uplands was delivered by an Upland Meadows brown truck, somewhat like a UPS truck now. The milkman brought the quart bottles to the kitchen door in wire racks and picked up the rinsed empties, which were returned to the farm's bottling barn for sterilizing and refilling. Every bottle of milk had a layer of thick cream on top.

When I was a teenager, I went to the farm to help during haying season. I learned that female dairy cows produced milk once they'd had a calf, and that after their calf was weaned, milking that cow was the only thing that kept her milk flowing, although eventually her milk would dry up. Cows were not injected with drugs back then, so they had to be pregnant at least every two or three years in order to keep producing milk.

Something else I learned was that most bull calves were sold to the butcher for calves' liver and veal as soon as they were weaned at one month old. All this information I filed away until one day I fell in love with a cute baby bull calf. I asked the manager, Junior Mace, if I could adopt him, and Junior said yes! I put some hay twine around the calf's neck and loaded him into the 1931 Model A Ford and drove home. Mom was not thrilled. I was not either as the calf got away from me and ran down the drive toward town. Mom explained the facts of life for cows. This calf would grow to be huge and fierce as a bull, she said. He must go back to the farm where he belonged.

So I took him back and Junior wasn't at all surprised. I did not eat liver or veal for many years, until wiener schnitzel in Bavaria and Austria won me over.

Granddad died in 1963. Upland Meadows farm and The Uplands were in his estate and to be sold at market price. Mom rented The Uplands for two years, and regularly asked each of Granddad's children if they wanted either the farm or the camp, and they all said NO. The farm had been losing money ever since milk had started

to be sold in cartons, making the bottling plant and delivery trucks obsolete. Upland Meadows sold the milk from the Guernseys to a plant that packaged it, along with milk from various other farms, into milk cartons, and delivered the cartons to grocery stores.

Eventually the Gardeners, a family who had known Granddad from Rye, New York, bought Upland Meadows. They made the farm into a family compound, building many lovely houses around the fields, adding a pond for swimming, and keeping the fields open so every house had a great view. It's still a wonderful place to visit. If I'm there by myself a farm truck will usually drive up to me to find out who the trespasser is, and I explain my relationship. "Oh, welcome back!"

Getting There
A Trip to The Uplands

My grandparents had seven children. A trip to The Uplands in 1925 in their Model T meant a drive from Whitethorn, their main residence in Rye, New York, in three cars – one full of kids, one with servants, and one with my grandparents and their dogs. The first stop on the three-day drive was in Millbrook, New York, where they stayed with Thorne relatives. Then to Saratoga, New York, and finally to Keene Valley. All this now takes only four-and-a-half hours on highways and paved roads.

Skipping forward a generation, I was seven years old and my sister, Cindy, was three, almost four, in the summer of 1948. In the early morning we climbed into the 1938 Buick convertible named the Green Hornet to drive to Keene Valley with our parents for two weeks with Granddaddy at The Uplands.

Like he did before every trip to Keene Valley, Daddy had washed the car and filled the tank with gas while Mom made sandwiches (on white bread with crusts cut off) and packed the lunch, including cookies and iced tea, into a metal cooler. We stopped by the roadside – more than likely a graveyard, as there was ample green grass and shade – for our picnic. There were no organized road stops with picnic tables. No restaurants or delis, or gas stations with food. No Macdonald's. It would take us eight hours to get there, even with Daddy's genius map-reading skills that he used to find a new shortcut over a dirt road, or a winding paved road that we had never been on before but was sure to save us time.

From our house in North Haven, Connecticut, we took Route 63 north to Route 22, drove north to Route 7 and into Vermont, made our way across the Champlain Bridge to Port Henry, followed a shortcut to Route 9, and then turned left onto Route 73. We passed the Bouquet River and then Chapel Pond, and drove down the two-and-a-half-mile hill past Roaring Brook Falls and along the Ausable River and into Keene Valley.

We turned into The Uplands driveway, and Daddy tooted the horn. As we pulled up to the front door we were greeted by Dicky, Granddad's secretary and house manager; Curt, the butler; Anna, the waitress and upstairs maid; Elizabeth, the cook; John, the chauffeur; and Dana, the caretaker. We got hugs from them all. Curt said what he would always say when we first arrived, "Mr. Thorne is reading on the back porch."

I raced through the living room with my little sister, Mom and Dad following, to give a hug and kiss to Granddad. "Oh, bully. Bully to you, little lady," he would say.

Curt brought a tray with tea and cookies and we told Granddad all about the trip. The bags were in our rooms and unpacked for us by Anna by the time we went upstairs. We were expected for prayers in the dining room at 5:30, so we quickly changed into dresses. We knew that Daddy would wear a blazer and tie, and so would Granddad.

All the servants would stop what they were doing and come into the dining room for 15 minutes of prayers led by Granddad. Then the adults would go to the back

porch and have drinks. Harveys Bristol Cream Sherry was *it*. No wine, no hard liquor. No champagne – even for celebrations such as a birthday!

My sister and I would visit Elizabeth in the kitchen. She was a terrific cook and the kitchen always smelled so good. On that trip my sister stayed in the kitchen to have dinner since she was only three. I was allowed to eat with the adults.

Back at Whitethorn, Granddad's house in Rye, children had to eat in the school room, with Dicky watching our manners. But at Uplands, if you could sit still for an hour and eat without spilling, if you could answer questions when asked but be silent otherwise, you were invited to eat at the Big Table. The Uplands was camp, after all.

Curt and Anna would pass the food to the adults first and the children last. Curt would then pass milk or ginger ale to drink. I always drank ginger ale as it was a treat. Mom never bought sodas!

After dinner we would go to the living room. Dana would have started a fire as the evenings were always cool even when the day had been in the 70s. Mom would play the piano and the adults would play pool or carpet bowls.

Granddad went to bed early and so did my sister and I. We slept on a screened porch, each in our own single bed, covered with a wool blanket and down comforter. Mom and Dad slept in the room adjoining the porch. It was called the boys room as it had held six boys – Dad and his five brothers. Dad and Dana set up a wall with two doors so that my sister and I had a tiny room for our clothes and Mom and Dad had some privacy!

In the morning we had to be dressed for hiking and ready for morning prayers before breakfast. Daddy always came downstairs in lederhosen, leather shorts from Austria. After prayers and a hearty meal we would be off for a day of hiking, a swim in a freezing pool in the river, or a trip to the Ausable lakes. Curt would have packed a large Adirondack pack with our lunches – sandwiches and cookies.

We each had a small tin cup. The water in the rivers and lakes was so pure and fresh, we never carried water bottles. We just dipped our cup in the river and drank. This all changed as more and more people came to enjoy the Adirondack wilderness. It rains often in the Adirondacks, which means the sewage from the campers who camp too close to the water's edge flows into the rivers and lakes. No amount of coaching or sign posting could discourage people from camping as close to the river or lake as possible, and so the water in the Ausable River and the Bouquet River and in all the lakes eventually became unsafe to drink. We carry water bottles now.

On our third day we took a trip to Ausable Lake, which is three and a half miles from the Ausable Club via a small wooden station wagon that eventually was replaced by a green school bus. But back in the 1940s there were fewer members, and transportation demands were met by a sturdy station wagon built up on a truck chassis. It was a bumpy (exciting!) ride, and beautiful.

As we bounced down the last hill, pitched forward because it was so steep, we saw the lake and gave a cheer. The Boat House was filled with Adirondack guide boats, some owned by members and some owned by the club. The two club guides would pull the guide boat —which looks like a big wooden canoe – off its rack, out of the boathouse, over the dock, and into the water. One of them would help us load it and then keep it steady as we lowered ourselves into the seats.

Dad rowed so well. He had been on the Yale crew

and won many trophies. Still, these boats are solid wooden boats, heavy when empty, and very heavy when loaded. I learned as a teenager how to manage them; you set your course and row with a shallow stroke just under the water, doing your best to keep a regular rhythm. Once you get going, it is quite pleasurable to feel the boat move forward with your heartbeat.

At the end of the Lower Lake we docked and stored the boat in a rack and walked the one-mile carry to the Upper Ausable Lake. There we chatted with the warden and told him we would not need a boat for the Upper Lake as we were going to swim and picnic at Shanty Brook.

Shanty Brook has large flat rocks and small deep pools for swimming, with a few slides between pools made of slick rocks smoothed by the rushing water. What fun to slide down almost out of control and splash into the cool pool, swim to shore, and climb out and up for another slide! Then we lay on towels on the flat rocks all warm from the sun.

Soon the basket pack was unloaded, and we ate lunch. Maybe after lunch we would investigate upriver, looking for a better pool or catching fish or tree toads or finding a piece of birch bark so white and unblemished that we could write a letter on it. The trip home was always a different adventure, but an adventure just the same. Maybe the wind had picked up or it was about to rain, or we met friends on the carry path and stopped to talk.

It didn't matter what happened, because it was always a great day to be on the lake!

The Uplands

by Richard Longstreth

Note from Phebe: This guest essay is written by my friend Richard Longstreth, an architectural historian, a professor at George Washington University (where he directs the program in historic preservation), and author of many books (look him up!), including A Guide to Architecture in the Adirondacks.

Thank you, Richard!

Like many Adirondack seasonal residences from the late 19th and first half of the 20th centuries, The Uplands has a highly individualistic design. It is conspicuously larger than most other such houses in Keene Valley (they have traditionally been referred to as "cottages" or "houses," not "camps" in this part of the region). In the extent of spaces it shelters, The Uplands is more akin to the huge, sprawling camp complexes on Upper St. Regis, Upper Saranac, Raquette, and other lakes lying to the north and west. But unlike them, this house is a single building, with a taut, linear arrangement of rooms on two floors. The mass is broken into two parts, one with a vast living hall; the other with dining room, pantry, and kitchen at ground level, separated by a covered passageway. Above, a range of bedrooms lies on both sides of the corridor in the first section and to just one side in the second. This division is found in a number of early twentieth-century Keene Valley houses, although the dining room-kitchen (locally called the cook house) was generally a distinctly separate building, often some distance away, with an upper floor devoted to servants' quarters. Such a separation made sense as a precaution against fire, but also to sequester the noise and smells of food preparation and cleaning.

This house is also singular in the character of its design. On the exterior, horizontality is emphasized, without the use of any decorative embellishment – rustic or otherwise. The composition is quite abstract for a house of the period, and clearly the work of a skilled architect, whose identity, alas, remains unknown. Inside, the living hall is one vast space, clear spanned by paired steel I-beams running north-south and east-west, which are tied to the timber roof frame and are themselves encased in wood. The effect of this space is at once sheltering and expansive. The ceiling is quite high, but seems low owing to the room's extent, while the perimeter is permeated by ribbon windows and sets of glazed French doors leading to a large, covered porch and the passageway to the dining room. The layout is nearly symmetrical, with a sunken fireplace on one side, but the feeling is informal, with walls of exposed studs throughout. The dining room is not quite as large, but retains much of the dual characteristics of simplicity and formality found in the living hall.

Sited on a plateau that was previously used as a recreation ground by summer residents, The Uplands once had a panoramic view of the valley floor and mountains to the east, as well as a more immediate view of mountains lying to the west. The approach is circuitous, winding through a tended pine forest. In recent years, some clearing has opened up the prospects somewhat, but the feeling is still one of a house in the woods.

Construction of The Uplands began around 1907-1908 and was completed in time for the 1910 summer season. The owner was Samuel Tilden Alling, who around that time assumed the presidency of Alling & Cory, a large paper-manufacturing company based in Rochester, New York. Much of Ausable Valley running north to Lake Champlain was being exploited for its timber at that time, and a sizable pulp paper plant had been built along that path in Au Sable Forks. Alling may have first seen the area while on business (well-to-do families from central New York were more inclined to retreat to the western Adirondacks). Samuel Thorne Jr., a prominent New York attorney, purchased The Uplands in 1925. He made additions to the service area and developed a model dairy farm some ten miles to the north.

Grandmother's Tea House

With seven children, and houseguests who often stayed not for just a weekend but for weeks, Grandma needed a place to rest and to practice the piano without disturbing naps. The Tea House was reached by walking around north of the pond along a lovely pine-needle-covered path. Originally one room that measured 20 square feet, the Tea House had double French doors that opened onto a porch on the western side. On the eastern wall there was a brick fireplace, and the northern side had a window bed for naps. The piano was tucked against the south wall under a window looking back at the path.

After practicing the piano, my grandmother would heat tea water on a wood-burning cast-iron potbelly stove that vented through the chimney. I am sure that Dana, the caretaker, had built the fire, so all she had to do was light it. After tea and maybe writing a few letters, she would lie down on the window bed and sleep for an hour before returning to Uplands for her bath, and then dress for dinner. She would have already had meetings with the cook and butler to talk about dinner that night and plan for other meals that week.

In 1946, when Dad came home from the war, he bought the Tea House, which was set on five acres, for $1.00. For the next four summer visits we stayed there but ate all our meals at Uplands. With Dana's help, Dad built a tiny kitchen behind the fireplace that was equipped with a small gas stove and a sink. There was an icebox that needed a 50-pound block of ice each week. This allowed us to have our picnic food and some breakfast cereals handy. My sister and I slept on the entry porch, which was now screened in. Mom and Dad slept on the window bed in the main room. Dad rigged up a cold shower by tossing a garden hose over a tree branch. It was summer and I don't remember anything but a good time.

When Dad was killed in 1950, we moved back to The Uplands during our summer visits. The tea house was not used until 1954, when Mom married Thew Wright. At that point she had a small one-room museum – which had been built for my Uncle Neale to house his rock and bug collection – moved out next to the Tea House to become a nice, separate bedroom for the newlyweds. My sister and I continued to sleep on the porch.

Thew and my mother divorced in 1961, and she moved back to The Uplands. By then Granddad was too old and frail to come to Keene Valley. Mom came for only a few weeks. She had gone back to nursing school at Yale New Haven Hospital, and she worked almost all summer. But in

1963 Granddad died, and Mom rented The Uplands from his estate. Although my grandparents had had six sons and a daughter, not one of them wanted a 14-bedroom house in the Adirondacks. So in 1965 Mom bought it "as is."

In 1962, for my 21st birthday, I was given the Tea House. I married Dr. William Hamilton in 1964 and we lived there, adding a bedroom, dressing room, and bath, as well as a new front door and entry hall where the old dressing room had been. We expanded the kitchen the length of the living room and added a door, so now there were two entries into the kitchen, one from either side of the fireplace. Sid Miller was the architect, and I am glad I hired him because it was tricky to add another roof off the original pagoda roof.

For a while the Tea House became the Weekend House.

In 1981, now with three children in our family, we added a loft with two dormers over the guest bath. The boys slept on the porch, the babysitter in the loft, and Helena (age three months) in the guest room. Mom had moved to the Lawrence Cabin in 1979, leaving The Uplands empty except for parties and guests. For four years, nobody slept there but visitors.

In August 1985, the boys each invited a guest, so we were three adults – including the nanny – and five children all stuffed into the two-bedroom cottage. Mom said we should move back to The Uplands. So we did, and I never left.

Again the Tea House was empty. I started to rent it to friends, and in 2015 I sold it to my good friend Jery Huntley, who added a new kitchen big enough for a long dining table and a wood-burning stove vented by the fireplace chimney. Now it is the Huntley Weekend Cottage.

Jery's son, Jay, is my godson, so almost family, and his fiancée, Brooke, loves hiking and being in the Adirondacks. It is a happy house! (Photo page 195.)

Adirondack Industries

In the 1930s, during the Depression, many camp owners closed down their houses and ended their relationship with their caretakers. So the men were without jobs, and there were no unemployment payments or food stamps or any social safety net. Granddad respected the creative talents of these men, who had always built guide boats in the winter or made chairs and tables for the camps they took care of. So Granddad started Adirondack Industries and hired these men, which meant they had work and they were able to support their families by building simple but useful furniture.

The tables and chairs in Uplands' dining room are from Adirondack Industries. A simple trestle foot on either end holds up a plain pine top about 22 feet long and 2 feet wide. There are three such tables, all of them stained a pale green, and 22 side chairs and 4 armchairs, all with caned seats, all from Adirondack Industries.

Upstairs we had bureaus also made of pine but painted white, with diamond-shaped knobs. Out on the porch were sturdy, square, wooden, painted armchairs. Instead of feet they had what looks like a ski connecting the front and back legs on each side. The outdoor table had only one leg at one end and two at the other. The table and chairs were painted a dark green that matched the trim on the house itself.

The men loved the work, and Granddad was proud that the business was successful. But as the economy perked up and houses were reopened or sold, and especially when hunting season started, the men went back

*Tables & chairs
from Adirondack
Industries*

to their old jobs. So Adirondack Industries closed down.

No doubt there are many old camps in the Adirondacks that have Adirondack Industries furniture, but I bet the present owners don't even know it!

South House

Across the kitchen porch, south of the kitchen, Granddaddy had a house built as the servants' quarters in 1925. It was winterized, with a basement and a big, coal furnace. The shape of the South House mimics the shape of The Uplands. It has the same roof line, deep eaves, windows, and porch railings. There are no blueprints. It was built by local carpenters.

The living room, which measures 15 feet by 30 feet, has a brick fireplace at the western end. Above the living room are four bedrooms and a bath. Continuing south downstairs is the bedroom and bath, and the boot room. Originally the boot room was a bedroom, and the door on the south wall led to a covered wood pile and then into the laundry, which had a series of soaking tubs. There was a wringer washer and a big, box stove for heating up the drying room. Clothes were hung outdoors in good weather, but when it rained they were hung up inside, in the hot laundry room.

Now in the winter we enter through the boot room to remove all footwear, and then walk into the large kitchen and informal dining room. There is a modern

*The South House
is the third building
from the left
(with six windows)*

stove and washer and dryer.

Daddy and his sister, Emeline, organized a ski week now and again when they were in college. The caretaker, Dana Lawrence, built fires in the fireplaces and kept the furnace going so everyone stayed warm. He prepared meals and in general took care of things. Those house parties were famous! All the laundry and clotheslines were taken down, and the porch tables came inside. A picnic table 20 feet long would be set up in what is now the dining room, with long benches on either side. Dana would have the room warm and breakfast cooking: bacon or sausage, eggs, oatmeal, cornbread. Then off they would go on their day's outing, but not before they let Dana know what they wanted for dinner!

When I was at Columbia University Nursing School, I organized the same sort of weekends. But Dana had died by then, and his son Kenneth was the caretaker. Kenneth was a great camp cook, but we had to appoint someone each night to shovel coal into the furnace at 2 a.m., or the pipes would freeze.

When my mother bought The Uplands from Grand-dad's estate in 1965, after renting it for two years, she installed an oil furnace, a big new water heater, and in 1967 a swimming pool. All those years as a child I dove into freezing water in a rushing river or one of the Ausable lakes to cool off after a hike. My mother hated cold water. Our pool even had a heater!

The main house at Uplands was always closed

up after the annual square dance on Columbus Day weekend. But we went up many weekends with friends or family in the late fall and winter to ski and snowshoe and ice skate on the rivers and bogs and ponds, or go sledding on the hills on the golf course at the Ausable Club. It was so important to take the kids out of the city and into the wilderness. We were all so fortunate to be able to do so.

What is a Great Camp?

In the late 1890s, wealthy families (Rockefeller, Vanderbilt, Post, Whitney, etc.), inspired by the Hudson River artists' paintings of the Adirondacks, bought land along the beautiful lakes and built large houses to accommodate family and friends who would travel days to get there and would stay for weeks. Because the local forests were full of tall pines and birch, the camps were made of logs, or from logs. Since it was easier and less expensive to ship boards that had been cut from the trees, rather than haul logs any distance, sawmills were constructed near local waterfalls. The very wealthy had their own forests, and their camps were large, log structures.

They were called "camps" because they were built in a big wilderness the size of the state of Massachusetts, and they were not the owner's permanent "home."

A typical camp had a living room with a big fireplace, bedrooms for family, and another building close to the living room for the dining room and staff rooms. The dining room was sometimes connected to the living room by a covered walkway or a breezeway, as The Uplands is. The stories of fires in the kitchen or in the laundry house explain why there were separate buildings. If one burned, the whole place didn't go POOF!

A typical Great Camp like The Uplands would also have a guest house or a series of guest cabins. A separate laundry house. An ice house. A carriage house or garage. A boat house. Hence the name: Great Camp. A Great Camp does not have to be on a lake to be great. But it does have many structures for various activities.

Lawrence Cabin

Dana Lawrence was the caretaker for The Uplands from the moment it was built in 1909 and occupied by the Allings, a couple from Rochester, New York, who were members of the Ausable Club. From the club connection, the Allings knew the Merlesmiths, who had sold them the 50 acres to build a summer "camp." Dana may have been on the building team as he was a good carpenter and problem solver, and he proved to be a good builder of structures.

There had been a pony racetrack on the land, situated around a 20-acre field that was used as a ballpark. At the edges of the field were tall white pines, but the field itself offered no shade. The Uplands architect, who was from a firm in Rochester, chose to build a house with large rooms and many windows and French doors, and with deep eaves that could provide the needed shade during the summer.

In back and to the west of Uplands is a flat parcel where the kitchen garden was planted. Dana tended the garden diligently and it produced enormous amounts of vegetables for the occupants of The Uplands. Dana also took care of the flower gardens in front of the house.

Sometime in the late 1920s, Dana asked my granddad if he could construct a small one-room cabin near the garden, and permission was granted. And so

Dana built a charming cabin measuring about 20 by 18 feet – with a fieldstone fireplace and an open porch in front. In the rear was a small galley kitchen and a bathroom.

Later, after Dana died, his son Kenneth back from the war, moved into the cabin and became the new caretaker. Among his many responsibilities, Kenneth tended the various gardens, both vegetable and flower. Although he was not a builder he could repair a broken step and fix a window quickly and well, but his real talent was cooking meals in the off season, mostly during ski weekends in the winter.

It was while working with and observing Kenneth that I first learned how to cook. Meals were simple but yummy, there was always plenty of gravy and a big roast of some kind. Kenneth made the best meatloaf ever. Mashed potatoes were from potato flakes out of a box with a heavy dose of butter and heavy cream. Peas and beans were from a can and cooked to death, but always tasted good with lots of butter.

And Kenneth would tell stories! His career on Broadway. His travels during the war. His observations of small-town life in Keene Valley. He always made us laugh.

When he was older, he found a nest of baby raccoons under his cabin. He raised them all and every one of them went off to mate and make their own lives, except Lady. She was attached to Kenneth and hibernated all winter under his bed. It made the cabin stink, but Kenneth didn't mind. In the spring, Lady woke up and began living outside, following Kenneth as he did his chores. But eventually she did mate and have babies. One of *those* became Kenneth's pal. This repeated and repeated until Kenneth became so old and frail that

Mom hired a woman from town to come up every day with a hot meal for him. Of course that woman reported the filth she found at the cabin, so Mom had the place thoroughly cleaned and instituted an absolute law that no raccoons were allowed inside. Period!

Kenneth died in 1975, about a week before baby Katherine was born. Nobody lived in the Lawrence Cabin until Mom and Chuck Prouty, her third husband, moved out of Uplands and into the cabin in about 1980. They added a large bedroom and bath with a dressing room. The kitchen was remodeled and made bigger by closing off the back door to the wood shed. The porch was screened in and a deck was added to the new bedroom. It was a one-bedroom cabin with two bathrooms. The old boat house had already been moved over to provide a garage. Chuck lived there by himself after Mom died in 2001, until he was too frail to make the trip.

When I removed the screens on the porch and also the deck, which was rotten and falling away, the lines and shape of the original cabin were obvious. But the cabin was unused once again until I sold it to my goddaughter and neighbor, Lise Strickler Gallogly. She has fixed it up nicely and uses it as a guest house.

The Lawrence Cabin is listed on the National Register of Historic Places as part of the original Uplands because it is still the same one-room cabin that Dana built.

Peter Thorne

My father was the second of seven children. His older brother was named Sam, after his father. Then my dad, Lewis, came along. Next was Ward, the third son. The first and only girl was named Emeline (pronounced Em-a-LINE in the South, Em-a-LIN up North), but they called her Emmy, or Em. She was the middle child between the three older brothers and the three younger boys: Arthur, Neale, and Peter.

The large painting over the fireplace in The Uplands' dining room over the fireplace is of Peter playing the accordion. In the background is the farm at Upland Meadows, and the surrounding mountains in the background. You can also see the old firetruck parked near the barn.

Peter was handsome, bright, and incredibly FUN to be with. He could play many musical instruments: piano, organ, accordion, concertina, flute, drum, harmonica, and maybe more! He had a beautiful singing voice and was a member of the Whiffenpoofs during his senior year at Yale.

He loved hiking and camping out, and all water sports. He was always thinking up something unusual and fun to do. The first time the boys went to Corliss Lookout for dinner, it was Peter's idea. It meant bushwhacking to clear an old logging road, and then a slow drive in the farm pickup to get to the lookout. This probably took a good two hours. Once there they built a fire to cook on, and continued to clear the view. And what a view! The whole valley lay beneath, with Noonmark Mountain at the far end; Baxter, Spread Eagle, Hopkins, and Giant mountains on the left; and Wolfjaw, Marcy, Porter, and Cascade on the right.

Peter never went anywhere without a musical instrument. Even on long, hard hikes he would pull out his harmonica and play a tune or two while everyone else was catching their breath. I bet he packed the accordion in the truck. While dinner cooked and they all watched the sun setting, Peter would sing in his clear beautiful voice, and everyone would join in.

For 65 years we and our friends kept the road to Lookout open and enjoyed picnic dinners together. It ended when the owner sold the land to a New York City architect who built a house right where we had always picnicked, and installed a barrier gate that nobody could get around.

Peter was killed the night before Thanksgiving in 1938 while driving back from a Whiffenpoof concert in Boston. He fell asleep at the wheel and hit a tree on Whitney Avenue, not far from his room at Yale.

My grandmother had died in 1937. These losses were almost more than Granddad could stand. He asked Dean Keller, the head of the Yale Art Department, to paint a portrait of Peter, the one that hangs over the fireplace at Uplands. It would not be Peter without the music, the farm, and the fire truck.

The purchase of the fire truck was Peter's idea, of course. Elizabethtown, nine miles from Keene Valley, had purchased a new and bigger fire engine, so they needed to sell their old one. Peter and his friend Fedor (Bubby) Smith bought it – for $25 each – and drove it along steep and winding roads, all downhill, back to Keene Valley. The brakes on the old truck were not at all reliable, and there were no doors, so it was a terrifying ride.

During dinner, Granddad asked about the truck parked by the garage. Peter explained that he and Bubby had purchased it for $50. Granddad expressed enormous displeasure that Peter had wasted $25 on a very old truck. It was a 1924 Ford Model T, which – besides the faulty brakes – did not have a clutch, and the gas line was gravity fed so you had to back up on really steep hills. It also had a tiny radiator for water, so it overheated quickly. The Model A had a clutch, better brakes, and the engine pumped the gas. The radiator was larger and you could go faster for longer distances.

So Peter told a fib. He explained that he and Bubby were starting a business with GG! The myth about the business soon became reality because the three friends decided to deliver blocks of ice for refrigeration to the camps in the mornings and return in the afternoon to collect garbage, all the while wearing top hats and tails with work shirts and shorts. I don't know what they charged their customers, but they had a lot of fun.

In 1977, Bubby's son, Nulson, decided that the Thornes had had this truck long enough and it was the Smith's turn. He put a rope around the front bumper and dragged it off to his house. But the truck was now registered to my mother, who had bought The Uplands with all its contents. She had registered the fire truck, had it repaired so it was drivable, kept it in the garage, and would come to the Keene Valley Country Club every afternoon in it to pick us up with our bikes. She drove it for many years, and I did, too.

Peter, Bubby, and GG were all dead by then, and nobody knew the real story except my Cousin Spike, son of Sam, Daddy's older brother. Spike remembered the conversation at the dinner table the night Peter brought home the truck, and he also remembered that Peter had told him he'd made up the story about the business because Granddad would be angry if he knew Peter had spent $25!

My mother got the truck back and donated it to the historical museum in Elizabethtown, run by the Essex County Historical Society. It was moved to the newly refurbished Fire Hall in Elizabethtown in 1979. To this day it is taken out for parades and other events. On the plaque it says: Given by Helen Thorne in memory of Peter Thorne, Fedor Smith, and George McClelland.

Peter's Cabin

The room that my father and his five brothers slept in at Uplands was the large room over the dining room, right next to a sleeping porch with two beds. Back then the bathroom had four sinks and a walk-in shower with two shower heads, one at either end. Aunt Em, the only girl, slept in her own twin-bed room over the living room, across the hall from her parents.

Being the youngest, Peter had been assigned by his older brothers to the last-choice bed. One day he asked Granddad if he could ask Dana to help him build a cabin for his own bedroom. Granddad said OK, but the structure had to be far enough away from the front door so you could not see it.

The cabin, beyond the garden and screened by a grove of pines, is small – about 5 by 9 feet – with a field-stone fireplace opposite the door. The two other walls each have two windows. I think the pine logs were cut on the property. So Peter learned about logging, along with building. He used the cabin with only a kerosene lamp for light. He had privacy and he loved it.

The cabin was not used after Peter was killed in the car crash in 1938 until the 1950s, when I and my cousins used it as a playhouse. My daughter, Helena, also used it as a playhouse. She and her best friend Sophie Lamount kept their rock collection there, and would build a fire and make tea there. But nobody wanted to sleep there. They were scared of bears and hooting owls and the dark. Anyone who went there always came back to the main house after sunset.

After we moved into The Uplands in 1985, I rented the Tea House to a friend, Andrea Robinson, who had too many guests one weekend. I told her another guest could use Peter's Cabin, and have access to The Uplands powder room and outdoor shower. He loved it! Many guests used it after that. When my son Lew married Bridget in The Uplands garden in 2003, they went to Peter's Cabin for the night. For that occasion I bought a new bed, but only a single bed could fit.

They said it was perfect.

Fillis, My Model A Ford

Fillis is a 1931 Model A Ford with a green body and black fenders, a tan canvas top, and apple green stripes and spokes. Her radiator cap is a bird in flight: an accessory that perfectly expresses Fillis's determination. Can a car have heart? If so, Fillis has one.

I have owned her since I was nine years old, as a bequest from my father. She was a real jalopy when Dad drove her home after buying her in 1946 from friends in New Haven, Connecticut, where we lived after Dad returned from the war.

Fillis had a torn top, holes in her fenders, and various replacement parts in the engine that fit but were not authentic. Dad bought canvas side windows and rigged up a heater, but it was still a chilly ride, so he wore a raccoon coat when he drove her. He filled an old doctor's bag with all the possible tools he might need for roadside repairs. As a doctor himself, he loved the challenge of tinkering with the engine. Dad always seemed eager to drive Fillis, and when he was behind the wheel he smiled a lot. Of course I also felt his happiness, and it stuck with me all those 64 years that I drove her.

When I put Fillis away for the winter I would say, "Thank you, Fillis, for a wonderful summer driving you." I looked forward to bringing her out when the weather warmed up. You get to see a lot more when going only 35 mph. You see roadside flowers, and people's faces when you pass them. They wave and I sound the horn: *Ah-OOO-gah!*

In 1967, I sent Fillis off to Page's Model A Garage in Keene, New Hampshire, for a total renovation. Every piece of engine was removed and cleaned. Any parts not authentic were replaced with Ford Model A parts. With new paint and a rebuilt engine, she was the best-looking Model A in our tiny town of Keene Valley, New York. We had 13 Model A's in town, as well as Model T's. Everyone loved old cars.

Fully restored, Fillis could go as fast as 50 mph! I stopped taking her up bumpy, steep, dirt roads for a picnic dinner; all those bumps would loosen bolts, things would start to fall off, and she would stop. Dad's doctor bag was useless in my hands, so we would push her or tow her to Carl Bigelow's garage. Carl took care of all the old cars.

Every Memorial Day weekend, I would put her battery back in, fill the radiator, then start her up. Down with the gas throttle and up with the spark, foot on the starter. She would cough and I would pull the choke and she'd catch: *chugga chugga*. I'd adjust the spark and gas back until I heard a nice *hummmm*.

In 2012, I shipped Fillis to Sun Valley, Idaho, where I lived summer and winter. When I started her up to drive off the covered trailer, she sputtered and coughed. I was well aware that she was 81, but she was behaving as if she had altitude sickness. So I filled her tank with high-test gas . . . and then she soared like the bird on her radiator cap.

Ah-OOO-gah, Fillis!

Thew

Mom married Thew in 1954 while Cindy and I were at summer camp in New Hampshire. When Mom arrived at the end of camp to drive us home and introduced us to him saying, "This is my husband," it was a shock. Mom had dated a lot of attractive men since Dad's death, but no one seemed to be a threat to our little family of three. Thew was a threat!

He was a well-known trial lawyer who looked like Paul Newman, with wavy blond hair and bright blue eyes. He was graceful and well dressed. There was no television yet, and the biggest entertainment in New Haven was to hear Thew's opening and, later, closing statements for whatever trial he was working on.

Thew was graceful dancer, a good golfer, and a pretty good piano player after dinner, although he knew only Broadway songbook standards. He was also an adventuresome traveler, and we were introduced to foreign lands and exotic vacations. He loved to meet new people and charm them and entertain them with stories and make them laugh. He adored Mom and she was totally smitten. He could do no wrong.

They had been married seven years when he suddenly walked out on Mom in the middle of a big party celebrating his 25th Yale reunion.

She was devastated, of course. But she had lived through watching Dad be shot to death and being shot through the head herself, so she made a plan. She booked passage on the Queen Mary to England, and then traveled to Paris. I was able to go with her as I had graduated from Bradford Jr. College and was free until September, when I would start Columbia Nursing School. From Paris, Mom and I went to Biarritz in southern France. She invited her niece, Carol Ann, who lived in Madrid, to join us. While the three of us were walking the beach one day, Mom removed her wedding ring and threw it hard onto the ocean.

When she returned to New Haven she called the Dean of Columbia Nursing School and asked if she could come back and finish her degree. She had already completed two out of three years of nursing school when she'd married Dad and dropped out because Columbia would not allow nursing students to be married!

The Dean asked her how old she was, and she said, "46."

"Oh, my," the Dean replied. "The cut-off age is 45."

Mom called Yale School of Nursing and told them she was 44. She graduated in 1964, the same day I did. We were very proud of each other.

Meanwhile, Thew had run off with a beautiful, younger woman who was an artist and wealthy socialite, Katherine (Kit) Dean. They had a son in 1963, Clinton (Chip) Wright. I always thought of Chip as a step-brother, and I enjoyed Kit's company, but I felt uneasy about Thew. He had left his first wife and three kids for my mother. That was forgivable because Mom was the tragic widow whom everyone wanted to see happy. But leaving Mom so suddenly, and again for the adventure of a new conquest, could not be forgiven. His law firm tossed him out.

Thew and Kit and little Chip moved to Cuernavaca, Mexico, where they bought a beautiful hacienda and partied with artists and writers. It was a fun place to visit, and over the years I watched Chip grow tall and more beautiful than his Dad, with perfect manners, and the same grace and talent for easy conversation and making people feel comfortable. He became fluent in both En-glish and Spanish.

By the time Chip came to the U.S. for college, Thew had dumped *his* mother for a young woman he'd met by the Beverly Hills Hotel pool. She had no money, so he started to write about his exciting law cases. But he couldn't capture the emotions of a single character. Nothing he wrote was ever published. He ran out of money and lived in a van plugged into an outlet on the outside of a house belonging to friends in Florida.

When Clinton had vacations and weekends free, he often came to visit us at The Uplands. Mom, ever her emotionally generous self, would sit on the couch with him and tell him about his dad and show him photos of Thew playing golf, Thew dancing, and Thew playing the piano.

When Mom was married to Chuck, Thew called one day to say that he was in New Haven and could they have lunch? With Chuck's permission, they met, and Mom told me they talked and laughed over lunch and enjoyed each other's company. He was a charmer!

Kit felt bitter about Thew leaving her, and would not allow anyone to even mention the name Thew. All the more reason why Clinton was desperate to learn about his father from someone who'd known him. At Clinton's wedding to Jeanne, I sat down next to Kit and said, "Kit, you and Thew are the mother and father of the groom, and you should dance together just once." She said she would, but Thew had to come ask her. He did, and after the dance they sat and talked. She ended up inviting him to stay in her house in Greenwich for a week.

When Thew died, we all assembled after the funeral and shared our stories. Stepchildren and children, we all forgave him for hurting us. Thew was a sociopathic lover and charmer who didn't understand the concept of commitment. He lived life fully and had lots of fun, but it never occurred to him that he was hurting the very people who loved him and needed his kindness.

Charles Newton Prouty

Charles (Chuck) Newton Prouty and Mom met at a dinner party in 1970. They were married at The Uplands in August 1972. He made a grand arrival in his new Ford LTD convertible. Cindy and I now had a baby brother, Charles Sanford Prouty. A graduate of the Naval Academy, Charles had been a Navy Seal during the Vietnam War. He was, in 1972, an FBI agent. He was married to Betty and they had two daughters, Ann and Maggie.

Mom had joined the Hillsboro Club in Florida and that became where we had our fall reunion at Thanksgiving. Every summer we would have a reunion at The Uplands. Our families merged well and all our children bonded and became friends.

Mom and Chuck had two big house parties each summer. On one of those weekends it rained and rained. Houseguests played bridge. They walked in the rain. They looked out the windows. They drank tea.

And then Mom and I decided we would put the collection of Audubon prints on the walls of the dining room. My husband Bill found a scalpel and a ruler and a cutting board. Someone went out and bought a box of thumb tacks. We were in business. We measured the spaces between the studs (all varying sizes) and Bill cut the prints to fit. I tacked them up according to the Artistic Committee's decision. These prints are still displayed on the dining room walls.

In 1982, Mom and Chuck decided The Uplands was too big to live in during summer, and they moved into the Lawrence Cabin. They added a main bedroom and bath and a big deck looking at Porter Mountain over a large meadow that was once the vegetable garden that fed everyone at The Uplands all summer long.

Mom continued to walk up the hill to Uplands to play the piano and compose her own melodies, to cut flowers in the garden, and to swim in the pool. Houseguests came for visits and we had family dinners there. Nobody lived in Uplands for three years. The summer of 1985 was the turning point. That's when my family of five – plus friends and babysitters – moved back to the big house.

Slowly I took over managing things. Mom was happy in her little cabin with Chuck. For a while they continued to have houseguests stay at The Uplands, but as they aged it seemed like a lot of work. Their friends were also aging, and for some of them the five-hour drive up and back was too much.

Mom died in 2001 of cancer, one month after 9/11. Her hospice took good care of her to the end. Chuck lived another nine years at their retirement community in Branford, Connecticut. He never returned to The Uplands after Mom died, but Chuck's son Sandy came. He joined the Ausable Club, so sometimes he would stay at the Club and sometimes he would stay at Uplands. We had two big reunions the two years before I sold The Uplands. It had been used as a family retreat for almost 100 years. Those reunions were a fitting end to the Thorne years.

Billy

I met Billy during my second year of nursing school, when I was working evenings and nights on the general medical wards. During our first year of school we studied biology, chemistry, and anatomy, and we nurses took many classes with the medical students, which meant that we all got to know each other. After work we would sleep late, so the first meal of the day would be lunch in the cafeteria.

I sat down at lunch one day next to Lewis Hamilton, who was dating my best friend, Annabelle. He introduced me to Bill Hamilton – they were not related — who was telling a story about his grandfather, who had attended medical school in Boston in the 1880s. When diagnosed with tuberculosis, his doctor had told him he needed to go west as far as he could in order to breathe dry, pure air. He took the train to Kansas City and a stagecoach to Texas, where he bought a horse and rode to Fort Stockton. That was about as far as anyone went in the 1880s. There he became a judge and wrote long letters home to his family in Virginia. From these letters, Billy knew great stories of Wyatt Earp and Billy the Kid, and tales of Indians and the Cavalry riding into town.

I invited Billy to Keene Valley along with Annabelle and Lewis, and we had a great time. Over the next ten months we fell in love, and were engaged in 1963. We both graduated in June of 1964, so we decided to get married the day before graduation on a Monday, when the Colony Club could take us and the band we wanted was available. It was a beautiful dinner dance for 150, and the next day, after our graduation ceremonies, we went straight to the airport to leave for our honeymoon in Germany. We picked up a little Mercedes in Munich and drove all over Bavaria. We were in Salzburg while they were filming Julie Andrews' movie *The Sound of Music*. What a beautiful part of the world! I wouldn't see it again until a ski vacation in Kitzbuhel in 1986 with a different husband and three children.

Bill started his internship and residency in orthopedics at Roosevelt Hospital on West 58th Street. We rented a new apartment across the street. On the wall in the guest room we installed bookshelves for Bill's extensive collection of very heavy medical history books. One night we were startled awake because we heard a huge crash! The bookshelves had pulled out of the flimsy wall and all the books were in a big mess on the floor.

With that, we decided to buy a co-op near the hospital. Every real-estate person I contacted kept showing me apartments on Fifth Ave and Park Ave. I kept saying we wanted to live on the WEST side! One rainy Sunday, Kitty Pell called. She had seen an ad for an apartment at 55 Central Park West. We went right over and it was perfect! If you like a place on a rainy day, you will be happy on a sunny day. The couple had just renovated the kitchen but they had a new baby, so they decided to move to the suburbs.

The apartment building had gone up in the 1920s. There were leaded casement windows that looked out on Central Park to the east, to a church roof to the south, and across the backyards with laundry hanging from clotheslines to the west. We had two big bedrooms and baths with a small maid's room and bathroom off the kitchen. The foyer didn't count as a room, but it held a piano, the 1701 carved bench, and a small Queen Anne table. The dining room was large so our little table from the old apartment looked lost in it. The kitchen also had a breakfast room.

I graduated from Columbia Nursing School in 1964 on the same day my mother graduated from Yale School of Nursing!

I worked as evening supervisor at Columbia Medical Center. Subways didn't work as well as they do now, and were dangerous for a female at night, so I drove to 168th Street in our little Mercedes and parked in the hospital lot. I enjoyed my work – the high drama, the multitasking, the triage challenges, the feeling of helping patients and their families.

One day a week I went to the Art Students League to take classes. There I met Valer Gordon and Mary Anna Voltz, talented artists who helped me learn how to paint. Soon the three of us rented a studio on East 83rd near Second Ave, and that is where Valer painted the vegetables that are hanging over the mantle in South House. Mary Anna painted the portrait of me with my parrot that is over the living-room fireplace. I enjoyed painting in Keene Valley outdoors. Many of my paintings are sprinkled around The Uplands.

One day I went down to the Henry Street Settlement and sat with the executive director, Helen Hall, and asked if I could help, thinking of course that with my health care job they would place me in the community care program. Oh no, they needed help in the drama department! So I assisted Joe Balfior, who taught kids from age 10 to 18 to work together and put on a big musical such as *Bye Bye Birdie*, or *The Music Man*. They not only learned to act and sing and dance, they learned to get along, which was important as there was still quite a bit of gang violence on the Lower East Side. I was there every Tuesday and Thursday from 4 until 6 p.m. When I wrote the Board of Directors a long letter with suggestions of how to improve the program, they asked me to become a Board Member. I said yes!

Billy worked long hours without enough sleep, but we still managed to get to Keene Valley whenever possible. We stayed in South House during fall and winter, and the Weekend House in the summer. At the end of his Roosevelt Hospital residency, Bill decided to do two short residencies of 12 weeks each, studying children's orthopedics. First we spent 12 weeks in Hartford, Connecticut, when he was at Newington Children's Hospital. I worked as assistant head nurse with a good team on a mixed-medicine surgical floor at West Hartford Hospital.

His second 12 weeks was in Minneapolis. It was late

fall, and cold. We lived in a room at a small motel. I did a lot of Christmas shopping at Dayton's Department Store. Then I found an old Bradford buddy who took me horseback riding in Wayzata, nine miles west of Minneapolis on the shores of Lake Minnetonka. And I found the parents of Helen Bradford – Gray and Bud McKay. So just as we were packing to leave, I was starting to enjoy it!

Back in New York, Bill started a practice with three other orthopedic surgeons. I so wanted to have a baby, but I couldn't get pregnant. We applied through Spence Chapin to adopt. In 10 months, in May 1971, the call came in and went to meet our little boy. Billy reached toward the baby, who grabbed his hand and smiled. Billy smiled back and said to me, "He's a wee Tad." Tad became his nickname until he went off to boarding school and decided to be a big boy named Lewis Thorne Hamilton. But everybody called him Lew.

In 1972, while still working as a nurse, I called my state senator from the Adirondacks, Ron Stafford, to complain that the D&H (Delaware and Hudson) Railway was cutting rail passenger service from Albany to Montreal. He was upset, too, and asked me to come to Albany every Tuesday to lobby for restoration of passenger service. He said he would give me a desk and introduce me to all the people I should talk to.

What fun I had, and success, too! I couldn't convince D&H President Bruce Sterzing to keep things the way they were. "Passengers are a money-losing operation," he said. So I went to Amtrak, but they said they already had passenger service to Montreal via Connecticut, and through Vermont on a sleeper. The New York Senate and Assembly members, however, were all for a train from Albany to Montreal in their state.

I found a study that showed most passengers to Montreal actually got off at stops along the way. With this, I argued that the sleeper car was not serving the Empire State or Vermont. Who would board the train at 3 a.m.? No, they would drive to Whitehall, or cross the Champlain Bridge and get on in Port Henry. Amtrak was convinced, and the first Amtrak train through the Adirondack Park pulled out of Penn Station in 1973. We drank champagne all the way there!

As often happens after an adoption, the mothering and the fading away of the panic that you will never have a child worked its magic, and in 1975 I was pregnant! Katherine was due in August and we decided that I would have the baby in Plattsburgh, about an hour away from Keene Valley, where we were staying in the Weekend House for the summer. I found a good doctor and had an uneventful pregnancy. Just about the day of predicted labor, I had a gigantic contraction; I vomited and passed out. When I woke up I was in complete pain. Luckily, Bill was there, and he called my mother, who was staying at The Uplands.

They put me in the back seat. Mom sat next to me, taking my pulse and blood pressure. Bill drove fast. When we arrived at the hospital 45 minutes later, the titanic contraction had ended and regular labor had begun. They put a fetal monitor on my belly and it showed a normal heartbeat. But they did not believe me or Bill or my mother that the first contraction had lasted 50 MINUTES!

Katherine was never able to recover oxygenation during the next 15 hours of labor. She was born navy blue, with a low apgar score. They flew her to a natal intensive-care unit in Montreal. I had a paralyzed colon from multiple blood clots throughout, and was put on bedrest, with heparin through an IV drip to try to dissolve the clots.

I recovered, but our baby never did, and our marriage could not endure the stress of caring for a dying child for 18 months. By the time Katherine died, she wasn't able to put her thumb in her mouth, to suck a bottle, to roll over. I nursed her at home, giving her water with a tiny spoon, and holding her often. She died in my arms on December 20, 1976.

The funeral was at the Keene Valley Congregational Church, all decorated for Christmas. The hardest loss ever to experience is the loss of a child, no matter how hopeless a life the child had. The loss of my father, my mother, my marriage – all of these were simple sadnesses compared to the emotional devastation of the death of my baby daughter.

I cried for three weeks before Julia Walker told me to go see VK, a psychologist. In my first session, I did nothing but sob. Slowly I forgave myself for my body's imperfection in having a titanic contraction that squeezed all the blood out of my intestines and my baby. Slowly I healed.

Julia invited me and Tad to Jamaica for spring vacation. Tad was just six years old. Linda Fritzinger and her son, Timo, also came. I relaxed and finally laughed for the first time in over a year. It took two years with VK before I was ready to move on.

And then I met Jim.

The Ice House

The Uplands was built in 1909, before there was electricity in Keene Valley. To keep food cool, 50-pound blocks of ice were cut out of the frozen pond every winter and stored in the Ice House, which had been filled with sawdust as insulation. Twice a week, a block of ice was put in a compartment above the cooler in the kitchen. Vegetables and fruit such as onion, carrots, and apples stayed fresh in a deep hole that had been carved out under the northwest corner of the Ice House. Above this small root cellar was an insulated room big enough for two blocks of ice.

After The Uplands was electrified in 1925, when Granddad bought the property, the Ice House no longer had a specific job. It became a place to store wood for the multiple wood stoves and fireplaces, and it attracted a lot of broken things that were supposed to be fixed but just collected dust. The root cellar became a place to store old cans of paint.

In July of 1966, Bill and I decided to turn the tiny room above the root cellar into a sauna. It was already well insulated, but it needed an outside staircase to reach the opening, and it needed a wood-burning stove and a chimney. And it needed two benches to sit on.

Our caretaker helped us. The staircase had a rope and pulls so it could be lowered when the sauna was in use or raised up and cleated if anyone wanted to go into the root cellar. This project, which took two whole days, was finished right before the arrival of our Fourth of July guests.

We asked a few local friends to join us for cocktails and dinner. Andy Derr had a house guest, who had just arrived from Sweden. We chatted and I told him we had just built a sauna. He asked to see it. "Oh, it's very quirky and not modern," I said. He convinced me to show it to him, so I took him up the stairs and we sat inside on the benches.

He loved it. He said, "Any Swede would be proud to have a sauna like this!"

Guide Boats

Before French explorer Samuel de Champlain discovered Lake Champlain in 1609, the lake acted as a border between the traditional territories of indigenous nations. In colonial times it was controlled by the French and the British. After the Revolutionary War ended in 1783, the Continental Congress, out of money to pay its troops, gave them land instead. The Champlain Valley and the Adirondacks to the west were pretty much empty of settlers, so the soldiers moved there with their families and cleared land to make farms.

For the Native Americans, the French fur trappers, the military men, and the settlers, Lake Champlain, the thirteenth largest lake in the United States – 107 miles long and 14 miles across at its widest point – was a water passage (or, in winter, ice) between the Saint Lawrence and Hudson valleys, as it was easier to travel by boats and sleds on the lakes than overland on unpaved roads. In this era the fur trappers modified their canoes to be double-ended in order to hold many pelts and furs, and yet still be light enough to be carried between lakes and rivers. By using oars instead of paddles they could row alone with a big load more efficiently than in a canoe. But changing fashions in Europe in the mid-1800s brought about a collapse in fur prices, so these early guide boats fell out of use.

As the Ohio Valley opened up, more and more farmers headed for the flat land and rich soil of the Midwest, abandoning their farms in the harsh climate and dense forests of the Adirondacks. Mining and lumbering operations continued to provide some economic support, but the real boon came from tourism at the end of the 1800s.

It started with the Hudson River School painters, who were eager to convey the awe-inspiring beauty of the lakes and mountains. Because there were no hotels in the Adirondacks, they would find a farmer who would rent them a room for the summer. Some of the farmers acted as guides for the painters because they knew where to find dramatic vistas or waterfalls, or moss-covered rocks under a cliff of dripping water. And when it came to getting across a lake, the old fur-trapper boats – with a few more tweaks – were perfect because they were light and stable, with a yoke attached across the center so the boat could be carried on a single person's head and shoulders.

When the paintings were shown in Boston, New York City, and Philadelphia, everyone with just enough daring and adventure within wanted to see for themselves this vast wilderness. Soon the farmers added rooms and thus became hotel managers and owners. They also started guiding rich city folk who wanted to go hunting and fishing.

Tourism inspired second-home construction, made easier because the railroad reached the Adirondacks in 1892. First there were campsites, then camps, then fully furnished mansions.

Of course the wealthy homeowners each wanted a boat of their own. They had to be beautiful as well as functional, so the re-fitted trapper's-then-painter's canoe

was modified again. This new guide boat was made of fancy wood – many different kinds – and varnished to show off the textures and colors.

I bought an old guide boat at a camp auction in 1982. It had been built in 1888 by a guide on Indian Lake. It not only needed to be painted, but one of the floor boards had to be replaced as there was a large hole in the bottom. Mr. Hathaway had a boat shop in Saranac Lake and off my boat went to be restored. It took a year before I could pick it up and take it to the Lower Ausable Lake for my first row.

My guide boat is 18 feet long and 20 inches wide, with a narrow beam so it is a little tippy, but so fast! Once I get it moving it just takes off. There is a very narrow keel along the bottom that keeps it true and on course.

I named my guide boat Flycatcher because it is fast and because the northeastern flycatcher is a Phoebe bird. Phoebes catch bugs on the fly during the day, and bats do the night work.

The Race

In 1997, I was challenged to a race at the Adirondack Museum at Blue Mountain Lake (it is now called the Adirondack Experience), about an hour-and-half drive from Uplands. I had seen a movie of an old guide who was rowing and winning this No Octane Race. He took four or five short, shallow strokes to set his course and then just rowed with faster and faster strokes until he rounded the buoys set out to mark the triangular course,

and then rowed steady for the finish line. I watched the movie more than once, and one thing I learned is that a shallow stroke moves as much water as a deep stroke, but the deep ones take longer, so the forward motion is compromised. Back to my lake to practice!

But I lived in New York City, our lake did not open until after Memorial Day, and the race was scheduled for the third weekend in June! I found a rowing machine and that is how I started to train. I rowed 10 minutes before work, then 20, then 20 minutes before and after work, then 30 minutes before and after. It made a difference when I finally got into Flycatcher on the lake and started to row.

When you put a wooden boat on the roof of a car and drive, the air that flows over it dries it out. These old boats leak when dry. A pint of water weighs a pound. A leak can mean an extra five pounds or more, which will slow the boat. So I needed to soak Flycatcher overnight near the start of the race course to swell the boards and make it tight.

When you row alone, you sit in the middle. When you have one passenger, you row from the bow. With two passengers, you can row middle or bow, the object being to balance the boat. With the bow up in the air from a heavy passenger in the stern, you will not hold the course. Another factor is winds. If you are rowing against the wind, you want the bow heavy. Rowing with the wind, you want the stern heavy. In a race, you row from the middle and hope it isn't too windy!

I won that race, and the next year Helena and I

won the tandem race. After the first or second buoy, the rower has to switch seats with the stern paddler. We practiced this tricky maneuver on the Ausable Lake. On race day I started out rowing, and after we rounded the first buoy I moved on all fours to crouch mid-boat while Helena walked over me. Once she sat and started to row, I moved to stern and paddled like crazy while also steering.

For the last nine years there has been a wedding or a trip or a family reunion on that weekend, so I haven't competed. But I still row as much as I can. I love the feel of the boat moving in the water early in the morning as the mist rises off the lake and the loons are still floating near their island nest.

Here is my rowing meditation: I slip my guide boat into the cool water of the Lower Ausable Lake and take three quick strokes to set the course. Usually I row 30 to 40 feet off the eastern shore under Mount Colvin, unless the lake is calm or the wind is with me: then I row down the middle.

I dip the oars fairly shallow and use a quick racing stroke, tightening my arm and butt for each pull until I have a rhythm like a heartbeat.

I sing to myself with the rhythm as I pass Fish Hawk Cliffs, Alderdice Cove, Loon Island (careful of the submerged rock 25 feet off shore), Big Rock Island, around Marble Camp to the cold fog from the ice caves, to the Lower Lake lean-to.

Sometimes I meet the loons, who are unafraid as they preen and dive for fish and call their loon-y laugh. Laughter is a way to sweep away troubles and remind me of the joy of every minute. Even hard times remind me of good times to come. If a ball hits hard, it bounces higher.

So when I can I row Lower Ausable and get fit and hot and calm, and I laugh at the loons. As I finish I approach the dock slowly, then put the boat up, and dive into the lake for a swim, all refreshed and happy.

Three Parrots

The first parrot was Dad's. His name was Cocorito, and he loved my Dad completely. He allowed Dad to rub his belly and his head and even under his wings. Dad had taught him to fly wild and come when Dad whistled. One school day in the spring, when I was eight years old, Cocorito would not come to Dad when he whistled. Dad didn't want to be late for work, so he left Cocorito in the tree happily pruning his feathers in the morning sun.

When I returned from school, Cocorito was still in the same tree. But clouds moved in and it started to rain. Then it poured, and got cold. By the time Dad got home and whistled, Cocorito was completely wet and shivering. His flight feathers were so wet they could not hold him aloft. He dive-bombed into Dad's arms, cooing like a baby.

Dad brought him upstairs and into the bathroom, put him into his cage, covered it with a towel, and ran hot tub water fast so steam filled the room.

Dad stayed up most of the night giving him water with a dropper. In the morning, Cocorito was dead. Dad cried and cried for hours, and nobody could console him. Then he went to work, and when he came home we all assembled in the back yard to bury Cocorito.

Dad was comforted by Mom and the memories he had of this special pet. Mom, on the other hand, was comforted by the absence of Cocorito, who had treated her as The Enemy, and as competition for Dad's attention and affection.

While Dad had been in the Tenth Mountain Division, training and during the war, Mom had taken care of Cocorito, cleaning his cage and feeding him seeds and fruits and nuts every day. For this effort, he tried to bite her every day.

Dad decided not to get another parrot. We had a dog and many cats. We were also a family now. My sister was six, so there was plenty of action in the house to keep Dad happy.

After Dr. William Hamilton and I were married, I asked if we could get a parrot. When I had walked the underground passage under Rockefeller Plaza to avoid traffic, snow, and chilling wind, there amidst the fashionable clothes and tourist trinkets was a shop full of birds. One of those birds was a double yellow-headed parrot with only a tiny bit of yellow above his beak, an indication that he was still young. As he would age, the yellow would spread to cover his entire head to his shoulders. He was tame and not too expensive.

Billy said yes. He was a surgical intern at Roosevelt Hospital with little time to sleep, much less pay attention to me!

I brought the colorful little bird home in a shoe box. But also dragging a large cage into the taxi. We named him Sir Winston. I handled him a lot and he became very tame and loving. But he never could talk very well, and he would scream when company was around. So I would put him in the guest bathroom, where many a visitor to that bathroom would be shocked – if I'd forgotten to warn them – to see a big green parrot peering down at them!

In Keene Valley, Sir Winston was always out in the kitchen hanging from a rope swing while I cooked and did other things. I would put him in his cage if I were going to be away for more than 10 minutes. He spent the night in his cage, of course.

One morning, Kenneth, our caretaker, woke me to say there had been a dreadful accident in the kitchen. A wild animal had gotten into the kitchen, jumped on the cage, and toppled it to the floor. A big mess of feathers and parrot parts littered the floor, along with paws and tail of the attacking animal. We determined it was a weasel. They will plot for days about how to kill their next victim. Weasels are skinny and can squeeze through very narrow spaces. It had been a hot summer night, and the big door had been left open, with only the screen door closed.

The cage was stored and we got a dog. But I missed having a parrot.

One Saturday in February, Billy said he was going to do errands. He came home with a baby double yellow-headed parrot that he'd bought at Blumstein's department store. I opened the shoebox and saw a large baby parrot with a fully formed beak and wings but a small body. He had no colorful feathers, just brown fuzz. Only a parrot lover could fall for this ugly bird. We named him Diablo.

We kept him in our bedroom so I could watch over him at night. I handled him often and taught him how to step up onto my index finger. I spoke to him often, saying only, "I can talk," in a very sing-song way. After three weeks he said it back to me! So next we worked on, "Can you fly?" That took only a week. Then I put it all together, "I can talk, can you fly?" In a week he said the whole sentence, but with a Brooklyn accent – talk was *tawk*. And fly was *floy*. Correcting his accent took a couple more weeks.

Soon green feathers appeared, and one tiny yellow

Diablo

feather above his beak. We moved him into the foyer so he could see me cooking if he looked through the dining room, and he could see whoever entered the apartment, and he could see the living room.

It wasn't long before he picked up, "Hi, yoo-hoo, I'm home!" And if he heard the doorbell he would say, "Come in! I'm home." Of course if I was *not* home the person at the door would start banging on the door and Diablo would raise his voice louder and louder, until the elevator man would realize it was the parrot talking, and not me.

I taught him to say, "Stand back, I'm an eagle!"

He would climb onto the cage side and bare his belly and say, "Tickle tickle, tickle my belly!" He genuinely loved to have his belly tickled.

When there was a celebration and we would sing the Happy Birthday song, he would sing along with us, but as he aged he would start the song too early, as the cake was entering the dining room and before we were ready to sing. For the name he would blurt out a word of his own, "Blarr a blarr."

Happy birthday to you
Happy birthday to you
Happy birthday dear blarr a blarr
Happy birthday to you!

He liked sitting on his perch without the cage dome over him, but to keep him from flying I had to cut his flight feathers by gently pulling his wings out and clipping the ends. Then I had to cut his nails, which turned into talons that hurt my hands. As he aged he disliked this trimming, and I took him to the vet to have it done there.

Diablo loved to copy all kinds of sounds, including sirens, buses stopping in front of our building on Central Park West, the doorbell, my piano playing, and music of any kind, which he would try to mimic as he actually sang along with the record.

In Keene Valley he mimicked crows and owls.

Diablo was never really affectionate, like Cocorito had been with Dad, but he was certainly good company for everyone. He lived to be 37 years old. He did not die of old age, however, he died fending off an attack by two West Highland white terriers owned by friends who had begged to take care of him while I left Sun Valley for Christmas with my family.

I had asked them NOT to let Diablo out of the cage,

because I knew they would never be able to get him back in. But they couldn't resist trying to hold him, as they'd seen me do, so they opened the door and reached for him. Diablo exited and sat on top of his cage talking away and refusing to let anyone get near him. He had a big beak and he knew how to bite. He had bitten me many times when he was scared or busy with his own agenda and didn't want to obey. So they left him on top of his cage with the two dogs on the couch next to him. Then the adults went to bed.

West Highland Whites were bred as ratters in the stables of Scotland.

In the morning there was one dead parrot and two proud dogs.

The friends said to me, "Oh, the dogs only wanted to play with Diablo. They didn't want to kill him."

That ended that friendship. I see them now and again in Sun Valley, and I say just, "Hi," as I pass by them.

I didn't even have a little body to bury, or a funeral. I wept and wept to lose such a grand companion.

A year later, I bought a young parrot previously owned by a professional couple who both worked long hours and returned home too late to play with Icarus. Parrots love being part of a flock – which can be a human family, or a jungle of other birds in a bird store or in the tropics – and they pine for company if left alone. Parrots get sleepy at sunset, which in New York City in the winter is at 5 p.m., or earlier. They wake up at sunrise. By then, the couple had left for work.

So Icarus was dying of loneliness, and to show his displeasure he bit both the owners, a woman and a man. They brought him back to the store and there the owner taught him to behave and step up onto the hand. Icarus stayed in that shop for six months, very happy being a member of the bird jungle he lived in. Then I walked in looking for a double yellow-headed parrot. Icarus stepped onto my hand and we both fell in love. Finally I had a parrot who loved me.

He was affectionate but also protective of me, and extremely jealous of someone else who might love me, not unlike Cocorito had been with Dad. Icarus did not have the mimicking skills or the intelligence to anticipate-and-respond correctly, as Diablo had. All he wanted was to be close to me or held by me. Nobody else. He would let me rub him all over. He would lie on his back with his wings relaxed and open and let me rub his tummy and the inside of his wings. He let me massage his feet.

When Cornelius (Neil) came into my life, Icarus had had me all to himself and he was jealous of Neil right away. It got worse and worse until finally, in 2014, after seven years of being threatened with attacks, Neil said, "It's me or that bird. One of us is leaving!" And he meant it.

So I found a perfect home for Icarus. My caretaker for The Uplands, Jeanette, ran a day-care for preschoolers at her house. One of her two sons had a good relationship with Icarus. The best part was the jungle atmosphere of the day. Kids would arrive at 8 a.m. just as Icarus was waking up and preening his feathers. All those children laughing, talking, playing, and singing represented paradise for Icarus. After lunch, when the preschoolers took a nap, Icarus took a nap. Then they woke up and played some more, and went home at 5:30 p.m., just as the sun was setting – just as it was time for Icarus to go to sleep.

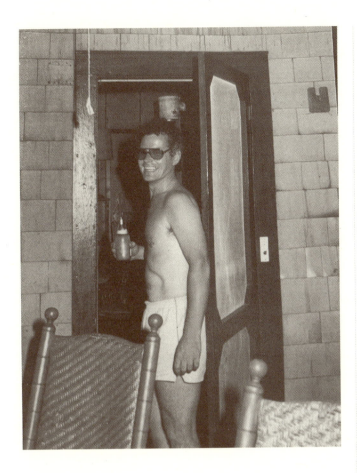

Jim Marrin

I met Jim in 1978 when I started working as a legislative assistant for New York State Senator Ron Stafford. I had just quit my job as evening supervisor of medicine at Columbia University Hospital, where I had been sharing a position with another nurse who was studying for her master's degree. She had no family and she worked summers and Christmas vacation. It was a perfect setup for both of us. But the hospital was now run by business-school graduates, rather than doctors. The boss said we couldn't share a full-time paycheck; we both had to work full time or not at all. They lost two good nurses with experience and passion.

So I called Ron and told him I had enjoyed working in Albany for him while lobbying for restoration of rail passenger service through the Adirondacks, and I was looking for something interesting to do. He said, "Come right up!" Soon I was helping with his Senate Higher Education Committee, traveling to Albany every Tuesday morning. I would work two days and return home on Wednesday evening. During the final ten days of the annual state budget session everyone stayed in Albany around the clock. Those were long days! Legislation for doctors, nurses, podiatrists, and dentists was sifted through his committee. I loved it.

One day the lawyer who ran the Committee asked me to take a proposed bill to the Bill Drafting Commission. He said I needed to talk to Jim Marrin, the chairman.

When I was ushered into Marrin's office I saw a handsome man in a very large office lined with mahogany book shelves filled with law books. It was impressive. I introduced myself and said I had a proposed bill from Ron Stafford. I gave it to him and he read it quickly. "Do you know what this bill would do?" he asked.

"No," I answered.

"It's a piece of shit," he said, and he crumpled it up and tossed into the mahogany waste basket. Then he started to flirt with me. We bantered awhile and he invited me to have a drink after work.

Two years later, on July 26, 1980, we were married at the Congregational Church in Keene Valley, followed by dinner and the first square dance of many at The Uplands. Our honeymoon was at Moonrise Camp on the

Upper Ausable Lake. After three days there, we paddled down the two lakes to get our sons, my Tad (Lewis), age 9, and Jim's son, John, age 10.

About six weeks later I found out I was pregnant. I was just starting my second year at Pace Law School. My baby would be born in April. I went to the Dean and said I had to quit but wanted to come back after one year. "You don't have to quit. Take easy courses. You only need 12 credits to be a full-time student. It means you'll have to take extra courses your third year."

So I did just fine and Helena was born during the Easter break. Five months later, John came to live with us. Oh! How happy I was!

When I went back to law school, Helena was a week old. The baby nurse would leave in a month. The woman who helped me with housework, Cora Mae, said she would help find someone for me. A few days later the doorbell rang, and it was Evelyn. She said Cora Mae had told her I needed help. I sure did need her.

After she'd been part of our family for about five years, taking care of Helena and cooking us fabulous meals, I noticed that Evelyn did not feel well. But she hated doctors. When I finally convinced her to let me take her to my doctor, she found out she had metastasized cancer. She died very soon after the diagnosis. I gave her a fancy funeral, which she wanted. We all loved her and missed her.

After that, Cora Mae filled in the gaps by picking up Helena every day from kindergarten through 8th grade at Marymount School.

I finished law school and passed the New York State Bar Exam in 1983. I then became an Administrative Law Judge.

Cooked Lettuce: A Lesson in Letting Love Find Expression

by Helena T.M. Grant

Mostly I remember my mother cooking our family dinners that we would eat promptly at 7 p.m. each night, gathered around the candlelit dining-room table.

Then one night, my father decided he wanted to cook.

Looking back, I imagine he needed a creative outlet to balance the stress of his high-pressure job as the acting executive director and general counsel of the New York State Financial Control Board for the city of Yonkers, a bankrupt neighbor of New York City.

That night my father had us sit at the table, and he presented our plates with a flourish and evident pride. Rather than serve ourselves in the kitchen, he served us with an air of childlike delight. He seemed so happy — elated, even. His shoulders square, his eyes twinkling, he took a first bite of his creation and made sounds of contentment and ecstasy.

His words conveyed that this meal was one of the best he had ever tasted.

I looked down at my plate and asked if the sad looking greens were cooked lettuce.

Unperturbed by my banal inquiry, my father responded with an elevated demeanor: "No, Helena — that's sautéed mesclun."

My resistance and uncertainty dissipated immediately and I knew, on the deep level where young children understand their parents, that diving in and finding the deliciousness of the moment would mean a tremendous amount for my father's confidence as an amateur chef-

Helena & Newell's wedding reception

in-the-making.

I honestly can't remember how it tasted, the cooked lettuce. But from that night forward, my mother no longer did all the cooking. My father's abilities and skill in the kitchen grew into a true talent and passion for which he became known and cherished by many.

And it remained, until his final days, his most favorite way to express himself and show his deep love for friends and family alike.

I think of that cooked-lettuce moment when my daughter, Belle, presents me with her latest drawing. Early on in her creative development I adopted the approach of asking her, *What am I seeing here?* before imposing my own perspective.

This opens a door for her to tell me what she wants me to see, a way for me to experience the artist's vision. And as she relays what the shapes and colors mean, her expressions draw the line between a scribble and a work of art – a subtle demarcation underscored by semantics.

Just like the difference between cooked lettuce and sautéed mesclun.

The Square Dances

Following the church service on the day that Jim Marrin and I were married, 80 members of our families and very good friends went to The Uplands for a sit-down dinner followed by a square dance. The band had two fiddlers, a keyboard player, and a caller. Nobody really knew what to do, but the caller patiently demonstrated the steps and timing, until we all had danced to exhaustion and heat stroke. It was a very hot night and many of us ended up in the pool.

The next year we decided to hold the square dance when it was cooler, so we chose Columbus Day weekend, and it became an annual tradition. Some years it was warm that weekend, but many years were cold and the fireplaces in both the dining room and the living room were blazing.

Rugs were rolled up so we could accommodate three squares from 8 p.m. until 11 p.m. While 24 people were dancing, the other 60 were playing pool or talking and drinking a lot of beer. I also put out pitchers of cider and ice water. On the two round tables at either ends of the couches were large boards full of cheeses and crackers and fresh apples.

After a couple of years, I decided to pass the hat

to help pay for the band, the food, the drinks and the cleanup. After a couple more years, I decided to support local charities and ask a fee of $15. That number rose with inflation, but there was never a drop in attendance. Over the years, young children grew up and brought their sweethearts and then their children. What started with two generations dancing became three generations dancing.

My daughter, Helena, was born in 1981. Her summer jobs were in Keene Valley, so by 1995 she knew every parent and every child in the Valley, and they all were invited to the Columbus Weekend Square Dances. In 2007, while sitting at dinner before the Square Dance, Helena jumped up and said, "Newell is here!" He walked into the room with his cowboy hat on, ready to eat and dance, and was not intimidated by 45 people staring at him.

One year later they were married Sept 6, 2008. The wedding reception was at the Ausable Club, and there was no Uplands Square Dance that year.

The last Square Dance was held in 2015, hosted by Helena and Newell Grant.

The Guest Books

My grandparents started **the first guest book** in the 1920s. It was black leather and the size of a large postcard. Guests wrote their names as "Mr. and Mrs. Smith," no first names or maiden names of the wives. They stayed for weeks! It took three days or more to get to Keene Valley in those days, of course, so a lengthy stay was in order.

Yes, they took hikes and they went swimming in the lakes and streams. But they also read a lot and wrote letters, and played croquet on the front lawn. And they took naps.

I started **the second guest book** in 1963, a year before I married Bill and was staying at my grandmother's Tea House (later called the Weekend House) in the summers and coming up regularly in the winters for skiing and sledding and ice skating, when I stayed at South House. Hence the guest book is titled: "The Uplands and The Weekend House."

May 11–12, 1963
Bill Hamilton and I climbed Giant via the Ridge Trail all the way – reached the 8th and last hump of the ridge and had to turn back – snow too deep.

We were married 13 months later.

June 16, 1963
Stuart Rose and Annabelle Gibson, Phebe and Bill climbed Gothic Mt. 2 1/2 hrs up, 1 and 1/4 hrs down. RAIN and BUGS: NICE.

A year later Stuart and Annabelle would be married.

August 28 – September 2
Labor Day Weekend 1963
This is the weekend that Lewis Hamilton met Kitty Bramwell. They married and had Heidi, who is my goddaughter. The entry by Bill Stason says:

Weekend launched with a slashing tennis match . . . afterwards a climb up Noonmark. Dewey [Lewis] near collapse but helped along to the summit. Happy hour gay as always especially due to the charms of two local lovelies, Kitty Bramwell and Joan Sabina. Good Sing Along at the

Ausable Club after dinner. Then a Beer party at Andy Derr's rocks til the wee hours.

Sunday. Shattered precedents by communing with God early AM then on to the Bouquet River upper pool for a swim and a beer. A great Thanksgiving dinner followed by indoor sports.

August 6 - 9, 1964

Cindy's 20th birthday.

Present: Michael Cusick; whom Cindy, my sister, married soon thereafter; our mother; and 30 guests. The following entry for that weekend was written by my childhood buddy from Old Orchard Road, Gregg Loeser:

Back exhausted from a trip to the Upper Bouquet pool but very healthy. We settled in for Happy Hour followed by a birthday dinner of 30 guests for Cindy. Sunday was a disaster until the 1924 Fire Engine was tuned up and took us all for rides through the woods.

To one who loves the water, the Uplands was a pleasant and charming change. Keene Valley is surely the best valley and the wonder of its peace captured the hearts of every guest.

August 17, 1965

On this day, CBS arrived to film me rock climbing on Noonmark. I had asked permission of the Ausable Club manager to land a helicopter on the practice golf fairway. Jimmy Goodwin, who had been in the Tenth Mountain Division with Dad, agreed to help with the technical problems. This entry was written by Rupert Hitzig, the CBS producer:

CBS arrived - complete with helicopter, many club fathers looked wildly into the air and gasped and shouted "It's a bird, it's a plane - no it's those Thornes again flying in for their daily golf game." Filming complete, everybody tired but great fun - thanks again to the Thornes for Keene Valley and its "simple gifts."

The air date was September 1965.

July 28 - 30, 1966

Inlet Camp, Upper Ausable Lake. Ellen and Dan Strickler and their children, Lise 4 (my goddaughter) and Tommy 5, Lewis and Kitty Hamilton, and my stepson, WG, nicknamed Double, plus two babysitters.

To get there we had to take the club bus to Lower Ausable Lake and then load all the supplies (clothes and food) and ourselves into canoes and guide boats and row or paddle two miles to the landing, then walk the mile of the carry with the supplies on our backs. A decade later there was a tractor, donated by a generous member, that performed all the heavy work.

Once at the Upper Lake, we loaded and launched more boats in order to paddle and row the length of the lake, about a mile and a half. We usually had a picnic lunch before the final sprint up the Upper Lake. We slept in a lean-to but there was a log house with gas lanterns, a gas stove, and a sink. A bath house with hot water and a shower meant this was glamorous camping.

Back in the 1960s and 1970s, the Club required us to hire a guide, who did the cooking, helped find the best places to fish, and cleaned up the camp before leaving. There are no longer enough guides, so we all must do what the guides did. Even the children are enlisted to help clean and pack up when we leave.

We climbed Pinnacle slowly with Lise and Tommy. Spent a long time on the dock sitting in Adirondack chairs, looking at the view of the lake, the mountains, water lilies, birds and watching Tommy and Lise trying to catch little frogs.

August 1966

Julia and Carter Walker came to The Uplands one weekend. Julia and I had attended the same junior college and both performed in school plays. She married Carter in 1961 and settled into a very large apartment on Park Avenue and quickly filled it with Carter Jr. and Lee Lee. After I graduated from Columbia University Nursing School in 1964, and lived across the park from Julia, we began to see each other. Here's what Julia wrote in the guest book:

Do this. Do that. Be on time. We had a ball. Invite us back!

And we did. They fell in love with Keene Valley and bought an old camp, Lonepine, across the valley from The Uplands. Julia was soon on the board of the Ausable Club, and we were both chairs for the centennial celebration in 1993.

The third guest book is lost or misplaced.

In the back of **the fourth guest book** is the invitation to an afternoon tea and piano concert in memory of Helen Ellis Thorne Prouty, Saturday, August 17, 2002. My mother had died the previous October in Connecticut, where she had lived with her husband, Chuck Prouty.

The fourth book starts in August of 2007, and describes a benefit for AARCH (Adirondack Architectural Heritage). We had a seated dinner for 80 followed by a square dance for 100. I was on the board at this time. In September we hosted another benefit dinner.

September 24 - 28, 2007

A stay at The Uplands for five days was an auction item to benefit the Community Library in Ketchum, Idaho. Lois Rosen was the highest bidder, and she brought three couples. Before they arrived, three cases of wine arrived from Lois's vineyard in California: Rombauer. I had never tasted it before, but I loved it! They were not an athletic group, but they were intellectually curious and enthusiastic learners. I took them to the Fort, to Lake Placid, and to the top of Whiteface by car. They walked into Keene Valley and shopped at every store. They loved it all.

Memorial Day Weekend 2008

On Neil's first visit to The Uplands he wrote:

Simply amazing – not just The Uplands – but "The Phebe," thoughtful and caring host, fun, loving, big heart, and my sweetheart.
    With love,
    Neil

Eleven years later, we were married.

July 19, 2008

The first of 3 garage sales.

Tony Pell came saying he wanted a pair of tennis sneakers to leave at his Keene house. He sat on the long bench with a dozen old sneakers under it and started to try them on.

"Oh," he said, "these fit just perfectly: like my old sneakers. In fact I think these ARE my old sneakers!"

I agreed they might be his, but since the proceeds were going to charity, I made him pay $5.

September 6, 2008
The wedding of Helena to Newell Grant, Jr.

The Grants had the rehearsal dinner at the Uplands at 6:30 pm followed by "darts and dancing" at the Ausable Inn for all the young guests. The wedding was held the next day at the Keene Valley Congregational Church. At the end of the service, Judy Grant stood up and wrapped a long scarf of Grant Tartan around Helena, welcoming her into the Grant clan.

The bridesmaids were: Melina Martin (Helena's roommate at St. George School), Kat LeFevre (who shared a house with Helena and ten others at Hamilton College), Elizabeth Fisk (who lived in Keene Valley), and Margaret Grant Mitchell and Caroline Grant, who both stayed at the Ausable Club with the Grant family.

The reception for 200 guests was at the Ausable Club. It was a blast!

September 26, 2011

Over and over again – 30 plus years of you and The Uplands, my respite. And every time I leave nourished – mind and body. I love you and Neil and can't stop thanking you for all the ways you have changed my life and Jay's.

Love,
Jery

In 2015, Jery bought the Weekend House (also known as the Tea House, now known as the Huntley Weekend Cottage).

October 4 - 8, 2012
Columbus Day Weekend

Dear Phebe, I had a great time up here for my third square dance. The Uplands is such a beautiful place and it is very kind of you to invite us year after year. I have great memories of this place, all thanks to you.

Love,
Conor Boyle

Conor would be my grandson when I married Neil in 2019.

June 1, 2013

Kimberly Cutter was married to Till Osterlund in The Uplands garden followed by dinner in the dining room. Kim's mother is Liz Stewart, a dear friend and big supporter of the Fort.

Kim and I loved every moment of planning Kimberly's wedding at the magical Uplands. The event was beyond the beyond.

Will Stewart

July 12 - 19, 2014
Prouty Reunion

What a wonderful week of family bonding! Hiking, golf, biking, swimming. Nat and I had a chance to demonstrate our canoeing skills and Phebe her trailblazing skills at Tenderfoot. All in all a truly memorable week. Looking forward to next year.

Sandy Prouty

And they did come in 2015!

May 24, 2015

Baptism of Phebe Eloie Thorne Grant, aka Belle, age 7 months. A mix of Thorne, Ryan, Boyle, Marrin, and Grant families.

October 9 - 12, 2015
The last square dance at The Uplands.

Hosted by Helena and Newell Grant.

July 30, 2016
A Toast to The Uplands, which received historic designation from the National Register of Historic Places, as noted by a nice brass plaque near the front door.

The designation also includes the buildings that were part of the original Uplands: The Weekend House, Peter's Cabin, and Lawrence Cabin.

July 10 - August 5, 2016
I spent 4 wonderful weeks here mostly taking care of Phebe-Belle, 22 months old. She wakes up at 6:30, but Helena tells me NOT to get her until 7! I have time for a cup of coffee and reading yesterday's NY Times.

At 7 sharp, I open her door. She is standing up in her crib holding KoKo, her Adirondack Black Bear. I say, "Hi," and she says, "Hi . . . KoKo."

She can walk on uneven paths up hills and down, but she wants me to carry her down the stairs.

It gives me time to hug her.

Fruit is waiting at her place and mine. I say, "Phebe Belle, I love you. Good morning to you. You look lovely this morning."

She smiles and says, "KoKo."

Then she sits on the high stool next to the stove while I scramble the eggs. She helps me stir the eggs with her spoon. After we eat she feeds Nellie. Then we empty the dishwasher together.

The day goes on like this; every little job, habit, errand is done with her, and I explain it all to her. She likes to know what to expect next. She is a sponge soaking up information.

I will return to Sun Valley and Cornelius, who I have missed. But then I will miss Phebe-Belle and Helena. And my friends. Life is complicated, but it is good!
Phebe

August 3 - 10, 2017
The final entry at the end of the Thorne era. The Uplands is under contract for sale on Aug 24th. I am here to deal with 100 years of stuff.
Phebe
The End

Family Dinners

Eating together is more than a feeding event, it is an important part of any culture. A mix of cooking traditions, memories, and identity, gathering for meals is a part of our heritage, and must be preserved.

At Granddaddy's house – Whitethorn, in Rye, New York – my sister and I ate our meals in the schoolroom where Dicky, the governess (and later house manager) had taught my dad and his siblings how to eat with knives and forks, and how to make civilized conversation. When we were 12, we were invited to the Big Table to eat with the grownups. Even then, we were not to speak unless an adult asked us something. Toys and crayons were, of course, banned. We learned to sit and listen and eat quietly.

At The Uplands, those rules were slightly relaxed. We could sit with the adults if we behaved well, following all the lessons Dicky had drilled into us.

Many years later, in 1979, the boys were 8 and 9. John was in school at St. David's. Lew was at St. Bernard's. Helena would be born a few years later. We had been eating all our meals in the breakfast room off the kitchen because it was easier to serve there. The large dining room was used only for dinner parties.

One night, after I had just served dinner in the breakfast room, the phone rang as it rang many nights. I said, "Don't answer it during dinner," as both boys raced to pick it up, saying so-and-so was calling to give a homework assignment. The call was for Lew, and he spoke only a few minutes, but it had interrupted our meal and stopped us from having hot food and a nice conversation.

That was the breaking point. There was no way they were going to learn all the manners Dicky had taught my sister and me, not with phone calls and interruptions and casual cutlery and plates. I announced that we would have dinners from now on in the dining room, with candlelight and real silver, my best china, silver napkin rings, and linen napkins.

The phone would be off the hook and under a pillow.

Slowly we developed the art of conversation. My husband and I started by describing our day. Then the boys were invited to talk about their days. At first, they would say nothing had happened that day. But as we, the parents, spilled all sorts of juicy facts and confrontations and dealings with people who were impossible, the boys wanted to share similar situations. Ah, ha. Conversations gradually became more fun and interesting.

I asked the boys if they would like to have a friend come for dinner each Thursday. They loved this, and so did their friends. A lot of their friends would say they had never eaten at a dining room table. They ate in the kitchen, as we had, their dining room empty, or they didn't have a dining room. A couple of times the boys asked a teacher for dinner, and at those dinners we all learned something interesting about history or math or good books or current events.

So now I have a new generation to teach about Family Dinners. I have a four-year-old granddaughter coming to stay with us for a week. The au pair will be close by at the Hilton in case I get exhausted. But I am looking forward to the challenges, and to bonding with this precious child.

Fort Ticonderoga

My roommate at Westover, Kitty, had married Tony Pell (Anthony Steven Douglas Pell) in 1962, one year before Kitty graduated with honors from Bryn Mawr. They lived in Washington, D.C., until Tony left the Navy and they moved to New York City, where they had Theodore (my godson) and Katie. It was a four-and-a-half-hour drive to Keene Valley and they came often. Tony's uncle and aunt, John and Pyrma Pell, stayed

at the Fort Ticonderoga Pavilion, built on the shore of Lake Champlain.

On one hot July day back in 1966, Tony and Kitty, who were my house guests for the weekend, invited me to a tea at the Pavilion. Although it was only an hour away, I had never been to Fort Ticonderoga, a large 18th-century star fort located at a narrows near the south end of the lake and originally named Fort Carillon, having been built by the French.

I dressed, as advised, in a flowered sun dress and a big straw hat, and my grandmother's string knit gloves.

The Pavilion, a gracious summer house, had been originally decorated by a famous New York City interior decorator, Sister Parish. It has a beautiful garden enclosed by high stone walls designed in 1910 by an Englishman, Bossom. In a small rectangular pool in the middle of the garden there is a statue of Bette Davis as Diana, the huntress.

The Pells and I entered the front door of the Pavilion, turned left, and walked along a long corridor with floor-to-ceiling windows that look out at Lake Champlain. In the living room, everything was filled with chintz: sofas, chairs, and curtains. We shook hands with John and Pyrma Pell – she was dressed all in white – and proceeded into the white-flower-filled King's Garden to sip tea and eat tiny sandwiches and cookies.

Soon the Fife and Drum Corps marched down the allée into the garden to pipe us up to the Fort for a tattoo, a short concert of 18th-century military music. We sat on little wooden benches and the Fife and Drum marched back and forth.

When that was over, we slowly walked through the sally port and out to a tall flagpole. While the Fife and Drum solemnly played "Taps," the flag was lowered against a backdrop of the sun setting over Lake Champlain.

After that tea and tattoo, I was smitten by the history and the land, and the beautiful Pavilion. From then on, many Uplands guests would accompany me to the re-enactment of the 1758 Battle of Carillon, or other re-enactments from the French and Indian War or Revolutionary War. I would usually invite about 20 friends, and we would arrive for the mock battle at about 3 p.m. While they watched the goings-on with Tony Pell, who knew all the history, I would be back at The Uplands preparing dinner. I'd show up later with a one-pot meal and set it up in the Log House, the breakfast/lunch restaurant next to the Fort with a beautiful view of Lake Champlain.

After dinner, each guest was given a lantern to light their way through the encampment with Executive Director Nick Westbrook as guide. It was always a magical afternoon and evening, and over the years the group grew to 40 people.

In 1988, John Pell died. Tony invited me on the board of a Pell family association that needed to be changed from a family project to a not-for-profit corporation. I had been on the board of Henry Street Settlement and chair of the development committee for 20 years, so I was generally aware of what my responsibilities would be. I gladly joined along with Peter Paine and Tony's cousin Ed Pell.

After a couple of years, I had a big idea: an Officers' Dinner in front of the Fort. I could see it as a moment in time. We would eat and drink as the French officers did in 1757, many of whom had their wives with them then. They likely would have invited settlers to join them for a dinner party, so we would be a big group, and of course it would be about raising money.

I pitched my vision to the Board and they were

excited. The chair at the time, Deb Mars, lived close enough to spend time reading through the diaries of soldiers and officers. She reported that the fort back then had had a garden full of squash, beans and peas, and a bakery inside the Fort had produced 400 loaves of bread a day. We formed a committee to come up with an invitation, a guest list, a caterer, tent rental company, and, of course, entertainment.

The Fife and Drum Corps, local high school girls and boys, played for us as the flag was lowered, and then piped us into the tent. The dinner became the biggest event of the year and was soon moved to a larger lawn in front of the Pavilion.

The Fort now has an annual dinner dance at the Union League Club in New York City. The first dance was organized to raise money to build a cairn commemorating the dead British and Scottish soldiers who attacked the French fort in 1758 under General James Abercrombie. After the unsuccessful blood bath, the dead had been dumped into a big ditch and covered with dirt, with no headstones or identification. A year later, the 400 French soldiers, no match for the 11,000 British troops, had surrendered to General Sir Jeffrey Amherst.

The dance raised the money. The ditch was identified. A large cairn was constructed. The annual dance continues to be a successful money raiser for various projects at the Fort. In 2009 I was pleased to be the honoree at the dance.

The Adirondack Pack Basket

The indigenous tribes of the Adirondacks used rigid backpacks for fishing, hunting, and trapping, and the women used them to carry small children. French settlers are credited with creating the pack basket that we recognize today. Originally they were made from black ash and willow, with leather straps, but now you can find them made of wicker and canvas.

The pack baskets have been popular for more than 200 years because of their sturdiness and usefulness.

They are easy to carry on your back and, when you put them down they stay standing up instead of falling over, as a soft backpack would. My Adirondack pack baskets have two small ash feet that run front to back on both sides of the bottom, which keeps the basket off the wet ground or bottom of a boat.

The Adirondack guides would use them when taking city folks out for a day of hiking and boating, and it's no wonder that the guests who soon became homeowners wanted their own pack basket. At The Uplands we had all sizes hanging in the ante room, from very small to very large. We could find one to fit a three-year-old for a picnic outing, one for a six-foot adult going off for three nights at the Upper Ausable Lake, and pretty much everything in between.

In Sun Valley I have one that fits my back while riding my bike to pick up groceries. It can carry enough food for two days. Everyone always says, "What is that? It's so beautiful."

It also turns out to be just the right container for a ride to the pool, or a picnic, or even an overnight.

Getting the Uplands on the National Register of Historic Places

The Adirondack Architectural Heritage (AARCH) played a key role in getting The Uplands on the National Register. AARCH had been formed by two pals who were neighbors living in rustic splendor in very old Adirondack camps near Blue Mountain Lake. Passionate about history and architecture and the Adirondacks, they decided to help save various structures throughout the Adirondacks that told the stories and history of people and places there. Over the years they have helped save fire towers, bridges, old hotels, libraries, town halls, private homes, and resorts. When you are on the National Register, you receive a tax credit for any capital improvements (new roof, broken chimney, that sort of thing). It comes off your taxes owed, not your income.

Richard Longstreth, a professor of architecture in Washington, D.C., lives in Keene Valley during the summers. His wife, Cinda, is a childhood friend. In the early 1990s, when my mother gave me the job of running The Uplands, the Longstreths came for dinner and the conversation drifted into a dissertation by Richard about the special qualities of The Uplands. Would I be interested in being on the board of AARCH? Of course I was interested.

Going to meetings, attending events to raise money and awareness, and traveling around the six-million-acre Adirondack State Park to look at structures worthy of saving was fun and rewarding. Soon it became obvious that The Uplands should be listed on the National Register. The process starts with the New York State Office of Parks, Recreation & Historic Preservation. We ticked off all the boxes and that part was accomplished, with the help of AARCH, in January of 2016.

New York State then recommended that the National Register list The Uplands. This was accomplished by the summer of 2016. A large brass plaque was placed by the front door. Also included in the listing were Peter's Cabin, Grandmother's Tea House (now the Huntley Weekend Cottage), and Kenneth's Cabin.

To celebrate, we had a party.

Phebe & Neal

Cornelius

I met Neil Ryan while raising money to build the Wood River Valley YMCA (now called "The Y") in the spring and summer of 2007. The Y was built the next year, thanks to the many big donors like Neil. In that year, I obtained a divorce from a short, very wrong marriage to a man named Paul Wilcox, who had threatened to kill my daughter. At about the same time, Neil's engagement fell apart. It was a mutual friend, Barbara Tamarin, who called us both to say, "You two will get along really well." She knew me from Lake Placid, where she had a camp, and she knew Neil from the Fairfield Hunt Club.

So Neil called and we had a few wonderful phone conversations. But I was about to leave for the fall olive picking at Kitty and Tony Pell's olive grove in Tuscany, and Neil was off on a trip to India. We couldn't find a date until December 27, 2007. I invited him and his whole family to come to my penthouse in Ketchum for a family dinner. My children were with me, but no grandchildren yet. Neil had seven grandchildren.

He called at the last minute to say they couldn't come because they couldn't find a babysitter for Riggs, two years old. "Oh, I definitely want the two-year-old!" I said. I wanted to see how Neil handled his grandchildren. He passed the test. He was affectionate and patient.

The next day, my children all left Sun Valley to bring in the New Year where they lived. Neil invited me to ski with him and his family. I must have passed *their* test, because I was then invited to dinner at a small Italian restaurant in town.

I spent a lot of time with the Ryan family until they all left to return to their homes in early January of 2008.

Not long after, my phone rang and on the line was a woman who said she was Paul's friend. Paul had left his rehabilitation program and retrieved his car, and he'd told her he was going to drive to Sun Valley to kill me.

I believed he *would* kill me if he had the chance.

I took Diablo the parrot to the veterinarian and left the two dogs with friends. I booked a flight for the next morning. I called Neil. He invited me to stay with him. I changed my flight plans and ended up staying with him for five weeks.

On Valentine's Day, a year later, he gave me a di-

Phebe and Neil's attendants were their grandchildren: Charlotte and Conor Boyle, Riggs and Pippin Taylor, Phebe Thorne Grant (Belle), Esme and Agatha Ryan, and Sam and Abby Hamilton. Absent: Frances Ryan and Perry Boyle.

amond love knot from Cartier and asked me, "Will you be my Valentine forever?"

Of course I said, "Yes."

In 2019, after eleven and a half years as committed sweethearts, we were married in a tiny chapel by the retired Bishop of Maine. Our grandchildren – Neil's eight and my three – were our attendants. All our children and my sister were our witnesses.

The first time I took Neil to The Uplands was for Memorial Day weekend, 2008. Neil's daughter Lisa and her three children were invited. My daughter was

coming with friends. As we drove through the front gate, Neil could see the house through the tall pines. "Hon, this is a really big house!" he said. As I toured him through the entire place, including the garage, his frequent comments were: "What a wonderful place, so full of memories," and "There is a lot of clutter." That was an understatement. In the next 10 years we had four big garage sales, but the clutter persisted. It wasn't easy to part with things that had meaning and held memories.

Neil worked hard with me to keep The Uplands in good shape. Every summer he helped paint the green trim, plant the garden and hanging baskets, rake and weed the driveway in front, fill the wood boxes, haul things to the dump, and clean and paint the outdoor shower. And he was a charming host for every dinner party.

But after spending more and more money every year to run The Uplands, and less and less time there to fix things and enjoy the Adirondacks, I decided to sell the house.

Goodby to the Uplands

In preparation for the closing up of The Uplands in mid-August 2017, in order to hand it over to the new owners, Jenny and Chris, I arrived in late July. The plan was to recycle or give away whatever did not have sentimental value, and divide up the treasures for my three children, my sister, and myself.

My sister suggested I hire Hugh, who had helped her move from a large house in Philadelphia to a three-bedroom cottage in Keene Valley. She said he would sell things on eBay, he would donate good things to charity for a tax deduction, and he would dispose of the real junk. Hugh told me to go into every room and make three piles: save, sell, toss.

Earlier that summer, in late June, I had come to The Uplands with a Sun Valley pal, Paige Poulos, to open the house and style it for sale. Six people were very interested in purchasing the property. Paige and I and my daughter, Helena, had put away family photos and all personal items, and we'd tidied up the kitchen, dining room, and living room.

Helena and I had cleaned out the garage and taken three loads to the Lake Placid dump – mostly broken furniture we'd always meant to repair, and a broken refrig-erator. We had planted the outdoor planters with bright red geraniums. We thought we had done most of it, and that the final move would be so easy.

So, now, two months later, we had a good buyer who wanted most of the antique wicker furniture, the Adirondack Industries bureaus and dining room furniture and porch table and chairs, the Steinway grand piano, and a few other things. I took Hugh's suggestion to heart and made three piles in every bedroom. That took one *long* day. Then I did the same on the main floor. It took three days to sort through music, books, dishes, paintings, and mementos.

Then I went into the attic. There I saw literally 100 years of clothes, old beds, old chairs, old toys and old dolls and doll houses, an old tricycle, a 1920s wheel-chair, wooden skis from the 1940s, a big parrot cage, old light fixtures, old sinks, old beds, et cetera. Sorting all of THAT took more than half a day.

My son Lew arrived to help. He sorted through and organized memory books from the 1950s through 2016. My sister was by my side the entire week, helping me decide what to do with this and that. Kitty and Tony Pell came every day with lunch and good cheer. A good laugh cures a lot of stress. By the end of a week of hard work, I was ready when Hugh arrived to remove the "sell" piles.

When we'd taken care of everything, The Uplands looked terrific. All the clutter was gone. Most of the furniture and dishes and pots and pans were still there, so it looked like a home. The potted red geraniums flanking the front door would welcome the new owners, and on the other side of the house the flowers rimmed the dining room patio.

The flag was up and gently flapping in the breeze when I turned back to wave goodbye.

The Next Chapter

by Jenny Clark

There is more than a bit of magic in Uplands, and the moment we walked in we knew we wanted to stay. It had been perfectly untouched, and so we could feel every laugh that had been enjoyed, every toast that had been given and every story shared in front of a blazing fire. We didn't want to change a thing!

Well aware that we are only visitors in the timeline of this great house, we just want to love it and see it through safely to the next century. Our first order of business was a bit like the scene in the Wizard of Oz, where all the characters get a good scrubbing! We refinished or re-painted only the surfaces that were in dire need of it, and always strove to keep the original color and patina intact.

Lamps were re-wired, outlets added, electrical wires replaced (safety was a huge concern of ours), and all of the rugs were brought to Albany for a good cleaning. My favorite part was bidding for antique light fixtures on eBay, having them restored, and adding them seamlessly to the house.

Every single floor received a "Cinderella scrubbing" as the caretaker and I called it. We were on our hands and knees for over a year! We didn't want to refinish the floors because the hundred years of boots and slippers had worn the wood so beautifully.

In the kitchen, we were able to replace the 1970s tomato-red Formica counter tops with the same toma-to-red Formica (the supplier called us, twice, to confirm we wanted such an "outdated" color!). We found one company that still makes fake-brick linoleum flooring, and we replaced the existing one for a near perfect match. There was a broken antique refrigerator about the size of a small car. Thinking of it in that way gave us the idea to bring it to an auto-body shop and have it re-painted to its original color. Fortunately, a commercial refrigeration repairman was able to get it working again, and just the sound of the old handles clicking shut brings you back to simpler times.

The massive double-oven cast-iron stove was clearly the heart of the house. When the Thorne family was in residence, it had been used daily since it had come through the door in 1914. Several professionals had warned us that it was no longer safe to use, but we found a retired schoolteacher in Massachusetts who had created a cast-iron-stove restoration business. He called this Glenwood model the "Cadillac of cast-iron stoves." It took an entire day for three people to dismantle it, load up the pieces, and then ship it off to Massachusetts, where after six months it was brought back to life. Now re-installed at the Uplands, the stove is safe and sound and ready to work for the next hundred years.

We found old iron beds buried deep in the garage, and with the help of our daughters we scrubbed, sanded, and re-painted them – they are charming! We had so much fun reuniting pairs of lamps and matching night tables that had been separated and shuffled around the house for decades. Beautiful, old, wool camp blankets and antique quilts were gently cleaned and placed back on the beds. In the dining room, the Audubon prints were photographed, delicately removed, cleaned, and put right back into place after the restoration was completed. The giant moose head was carefully groomed and returned to his rightful place overlooking his domain.

The true heroes were the contractor, carpenters, painters, and electricians. The head carpenter re-paneled every exterior wall inside the now winterized house, and his brother and nephew put at least four coats of tinted oil on every single board, precisely matching the original walls. The two electricians (brothers) worked tirelessly for two years to rewire the house and keep it safe. The exterior painters took incredible care to properly prep, clean, and restore surfaces before painting them – it was a dream team, perfectly put together by our "can do" contractor, who built a basement under all of it!

We feel incredibly fortunate and honored to have been able to embark on this journey. The Thorne family had protected this amazing piece of treasured, Adirondack history for generations, and hopefully we'll be able to do the same.

In the meantime, I'm gonna get cooking!

Contractor: Scott McClelland
Caretakers: Janette and Gavin Isham
Head carpenter: Pat Parrow
Carpenters: Kevin Parrow (Pat's brother)
           Colby Parrow (Kevin's son)
Electricians: Hank Auer and Harry Auer
Painters: Kasey Mckenna, Jeff Wade, and Steve Sweatt

Part II: Camp Cooking & Entertaining

Camp Cooking

18th-century Chinese Army teapot with drawing of Lewis Thorne in background

Camp cooking is simple meals pulled off after spending the day hiking or boating or skiing. By having a well-stocked kitchen that is organized for production, the ballet of cooking and prepping is easy. Steps are saved, time is saved, and the result is beautiful.

When I was a young bride, I went to Michael Field's cooking school. I chose Michael because he taught eight of us how to plan and cook an entire meal, and then we ate it! The assignment was to go home and cook it for our family.

While at cooking school I learned to balance complicated with easy when planning menus, and that has served me well when entertaining. If I decide to do an elaborate dessert, I will serve a simple roast or sautéed meat. If a soup takes time to prepare, I put a bunch of watercress on the plate instead of making a complicated salad or vegetable.

Over the years, I've also learned it's very helpful while planning a meal, to think about the leftovers and what you can do with them. For example, if you're having a chicken dinner, you can use the chicken carcass for chicken stock (the basis of all great soups) and a chicken pot pie. So you'll want to have a piecrust, carrots, peas, and onions on hand for that pie.

Most of the recipes in the book offer simple ways of cooking, with a few tricks to make them seem gourmet. I find that following some basic guidelines always yields good results. Any recipe is better if good ingredients are used: use fresh herbs whenever possible; use the best olive oil; cook with good wine; use ripe fruit and vegetables (but it's better to use stewed canned tomatoes than those hard yellow "fresh" ones; and frozen or even canned corn is better than tough, old corn on the cob).

In addition to recipes, I also wanted to share information on how to get organized. This book will give you guidance on running an efficient kitchen, and a "master plan" for pulling off a successful house party weekend, complete with shopping list and timetable for meal preparation.

Then to get you started, I give you menus and recipes for six different complete dinners, as well as a timetable for what to do when, and a list of possible leftover dishes that can be served throughout the weekend.

Camp is casual, so a camp dinner does not have to be a "soup to nuts" production. Following the six dinners, the rest of the book offers recipes for all courses, so as you plan your menus, you can pick and choose as the occasion dictates.

As I wrote down all my recipes, I realized that I had been cooking and entertaining at The Uplands for over 40 years. Some dinners were for six of us, some were grand musical events followed by dinner for 100 – they were all great meals, shared with friends and family in a very special place. I hope you will enjoy preparing and serving these dishes as much as I have.

KITCHEN SETUP

You do not need a designer kitchen to cook well. The best meals come from good ingredients, not fancy stoves or countertops. All you need is a good oven and two burners, a sink, and one work space – either a counter or tabletop.

The center of the kitchen is the sink not the stove. You will spend more time washing vegetables and dishes than stirring pots at the stove. If you have anything to say about the kitchen design, put the sink where you can see out – either outside or into the family room. The best kitchen I ever had was small but efficient space with all the appliances on the same side and a big butcher block counter across from them. I could reach everything in one step and had plenty of work space. Here are some tips for setting up an efficient kitchen.

- ◆ Put your dishes above the dishwasher so unloading is easy.
- ◆ Put cooking spoons, whisks, and other large utensils in a big vase by the stove or in the drawer beside it.
- ◆ Hang the pots and pans you use most often above your work space.
- ◆ Keep your spices next to the stove where you will use them, but not above the stove where they will just dry out from the heat.
- ◆ Keep flour and sugar in glass jars or covered ceramic containers on the counter near the work space. You will be reaching for these often and don't want to have to open and close a bag each time.

That's it. It's simple!

Pots and Pans

This is a list of necessary pots, pans, and utensils that should be in every kitchen. One of my most valuable pans is a 12-inch cast-iron skillet. I cook bacon in it, I sauté meat in it, I start the chicken pot pie in it, I bake corn bread in it. I use it so much, I never put it away. I rinse it, wipe it with a paper towel, and put it back on the stove.

Cast-iron skillet and lid to fit it	2 large, heavy, tall soup pots that you will use for soups, jams, and boiling jars for the jams
I small saucepan	
I three-quart saucepan	

The Uplands butler pantry

Sauté pan with 3-inch sides and a lid

Large roasting pan

2 cookie sheets

2 pie pans

2 glass lasagna pans

Large colander

Medium strainer

Teapot

2 ovenproof bowls – you can bake, serve, and mix in them

2 measuring cups

Measuring spoons

3 wooden spoons

Ladle

Knives: Chef's knife, bread knife, 6 serrated steak knives (also useful for peeling and cutting)

Vegetable peeler

Tongs

2 spatulas

2 wire whisks, 1 large, 1 medium size

2 large metal spoons

Slotted spoon

Cutting board

Staples to Have on Hand

Following is a list of items you should have for a well-stocked kitchen. Without buying another thing you can pull together many last-minute dishes: you can make cheese doodles on the spur of the moment; spaghetti carbonara with the bacon, or a tomato sauce; you can make tiramisu with the pound cake or bread pudding with the sliced bread; you can make corn bread for breakfast or blueberry muffins; you can serve the spinach as a vegetable course or use it to make a quiche. You can even make a curry with the shrimp.

IN THE PANTRY

Sugar

Flour

Herbs: basil, rosemary, thyme, oregano, curry powder, Old Bay seasoning

Spices: cinnamon, cumin, nutmeg, tumeric, vanilla extract

Onions

Garlic

An apple or two

Pasta – various sizes

Rice

Almonds

Raisins

Coffee

Cornmeal

Blueberry muffin mix

Brownie mix

Chocolate syrup

Chicken broth

Coconut milk

Vegetable broth

Stewed tomatoes

Tomato paste

Knox gelatin

Olive oil

Balsamic vinegar

Red wine vinegar

IN THE REFRIGERATOR

Bacon

Butter

Eggs

Milk

Cream

Cheddar cheese

Parmesan cheese

Mayonnaise

Dijon mustard

Ketchup

IN THE FREEZER

Ice cream

Frozen spinach

Frozen corn

2 piecrusts

Puff pastry sheets

Loaf of sliced bread

Sara Lee pound cake

Bag of shrimp

HOUSEGUESTS & HOUSE PARTIES THEN & NOW

When my grandparents had houseguests, they would arrive after an overnight train ride from Grand Central Station, New York, to Westport, New York. Or they would drive for two days, until the 1940s when roads were improved and car engines were stronger. A guest would stay for at least a week. My mother recalled arriving at The Uplands as my father's fiancée in July 1938. The grounds were impeccable, the house stately. My father showed her to the guest room where she washed her face and combed her hair for tea, which was waiting on the back porch overlooking Porter Mountain. My grandmother was not alive. My grandfather was still at the farm, which supplied all the milk for the Ausable Valley. He would rather milk cows than hike or play golf or tennis or fish. He was driven to the farm every morning and picked up every afternoon by his chauffeur, John. It was an amusing sight to see dapper, stiff Granddad being driven by a chauffeur in an old farm pickup truck.

The butler, Cort, served tea and cookies. Then Daddy walked Mom around the grounds to the vegetable garden, the flower garden, and Grandmother's Tea House – later expanded and called the Weekend House. At 5 PM, Granddad arrived home and washed up for dinner.

Everyone changed for dinner. While tuxedos were still expected for dinner in Rye (New York), where my father grew up, a more casual dress was allowed at "camp." My mother wore a simple cotton summer dress with a sweater. Prayers were at 5:30 and EVERYONE was expected – staff, family, and guests. Cocktails were at 6 PM on the porch, where only a small glass of sherry was served with some nuts. There was no champagne for the fiancée!

Dinner was served at 7 PM in the dining room. A typical menu would be:

> Cold Elderberry Soup
> Roast Beef with Horseradish Sauce
> Yorkshire Pudding
> Mashed Potatoes
> Fresh String Beans
> Berry Pie

Wine was not served for dinner. Cort would ask you, "Would you like ginger ale or milk?"

Cort and Anna served the dinner. Elizabeth, the cook, stayed in the kitchen cooking and washing pots. Cort and Anna would wash all our dishes. A dishwasher was not installed until 1965.

After dinner, Daddy and his siblings and Mom played pool and carpet bowls and sang old Yale songs around the piano. Everyone was musical, and as a gifted pianist Mom fit right in. The fires were lit both in the dining room for dinner and in the living room for after dinner; even in July and August, it gets cool in the evening. As the family left for bed one by one, Mom and Dad sat in front of the fire on large cushions and planned their excursion into the Adirondack wilderness for the next day.

My mother loved the trip to the lake, but the next day, Daddy ran her up one of the high peaks and that almost broke the engagement! Mom never liked hiking after that. Daddy never stopped, but he also played tennis and golf with Mom. My grandfather had his farm, and my mother had all the other activities of the Adirondacks. You don't *have* to go on a trip or play games. It's OK to sit in a rocker and read a book.

In 1938, my mother dressed for the day before leaving her room. For a day at the lakes, she wore long, full shorts that looked like today's skirt.

Prayers were at 7:30 and breakfast was served in the dining room at 8 AM: fresh berries, eggs and bacon, corn bread, coffee and tea.

Cort made the lunch and packed it into an Adirondack pack basket for Mom and Dad's trip to the lakes. They loaded the basket, sweaters, swimsuits, and towels into the Model T Ford (14 years old at that time) and drove to the club, where they took the bus to the lake (the "bus" was a horse-drawn wagon until after the war).

When I brought my husband to The Uplands for the first time, he was invited to participate in a full range of activities over the weekend, known in the Adirondacks as "The Full Pull." He climbed a mountain, paddled the lake, caught a fish and cooked it for breakfast, swam, played golf and tennis, and weeded the garden. He then helped me prepare to entertain and cook for 20 guests who were anxious to meet him, and he did it with a smile. He passed the test just as my mother had many years before.

Life at The Uplands today is not so different. But we have no cook, butler, or waitress. Guests usually stay only for a weekend. We have a dishwasher, a microwave on top of the old cookstove, and push-button phones, but guests are still greeted with tea if they arrive between 3 and 5 PM.

Breakfast is the same menu, but I cook it and it's served in the kitchen. Guests are encouraged to come down in their bathrobes. In fact, all the guests get a kimono with their towels.

We gave up the prayers and meet for cocktails at 6 PM. Of course we serve wine and champagne for any good reason right through dinner. We still play pool and carpet bowls and sing around the piano and sit by the fire to plan the activities for the next day.

We still use the pack baskets for picnic trips (except long hikes) and we still drive old cars and take the club bus to the lakes; it looks like a green school bus now.

One reason we and the guests are so charmed by the Adirondacks and staying in an old camp, is the feeling of timelessness. It hasn't changed much. Yes, servants are scarce, but we use the same dishes, look at the same photos and mountain views, hike the same trails, row the lake in the same boats, and sit around the fire after a full day and plan another.

It's comforting to hear and feel the thundering quiet of the past.

Organizing a House Party Weekend

Two couples are coming Friday night in time for dinner and will leave after a big lunch on Sunday. Here's my "master plan" for organizing the weekend.

I start by taking an 8.5 x 11 piece of paper and drawing a line down the middle. On the left side are the menus and on the right is the shopping list if the item is not mentioned on the left.

Of course, you have to plan and shop before everyone arrives. I do it on Friday morning. I start preparing the evening meal about 3 PM. In this case, I have invited extra guests for dinner on Saturday so there will be 12 for that meal.

Guests always ask "What can I bring?" If they are like my friend Beatrice Bardin, they will bring a whole meal, but usually I ask them to bring the appetizers or

Shopping List

Friday Dinner
Roast chicken
Cranberry compote
Rice
Roasted vegetables
Strawberry shortcake (3 baskets)
Cheese doodles
  for appetizers

Wine and beer, tonic
4 pounds butter
1 orange
1 gallon milk
2 green peppers
1 squash
3 onions
Broccoli

Saturday Breakfast
Sausage
3 dozen eggs
Muffins
3 grapefruit

Garlic
Bisquick
Heavy cream
Soy sauce
Tea, coffee
Sugar

Saturday Lunch at the Lakes
Chicken sandwiches
Fruit
Cookies

Bread for sandwiches
Mayonnaise
Carrots
Cherry tomatoe

Saturday Dinner for 12
Poached Salmon
Hollandaise – 12 eggs
Asparagus – 4 bunches
Baked apples – 12
Apple pies – 2
Guests will bring appetizers

Chives
Dill
Rosemary
Thyme
White vinegar
Almonds
Raisins
2 piecrusts
Lemons

Sunday Breakfast
French toast
Bacon
Fruit – bananas, berries,
  and apples

Cinnamon, nutmeg
Vanilla extract
Maple syrup
2 loaves French
  bread

Sunday Lunch at 2 PM
Salmon mousse
Green salad
Chicken salad
Hard rolls or fresh bread
Plate of cheese – guests will bring
Fruit and cookies

Lemonade
Olive oil
Dijon mustard
Knox gelatin
Walnuts
Grapes
Flour & yeast
  (if baking bread)

Everyone leaves @ 3 PM!

the cheeses we will need for Sunday brunch. Just in case there is a last minute shortage, I always keep a cheese doodle mix in the refrigerator and a loaf of white bread in the freezer. I also have nuts and olives on hand as well as carrots and cherry tomatoes to dip into ranch dressing. I keep a cucumber handy as well. This makes a yummy presentation on rounds of white bread with mayonnaise and it is also good in the chicken sandwiches.

The Timetable

Friday

MORNING: Shop for weekend

MIDDAY: Play

3:00   **Start prep work**
- ◆ **Fill the sink with cold water and wash the vegetables and the strawberries.**
- ◆ **Prepare the shortcake: Drain the berries and slice them into a glass bowl. Sprinkle the sugar and cinnamon over them and place on the sideboard. Make the six biscuits according to the directions on the Bisquick box.**
- ◆ **Prepare the vegetables: Depending on what vegetables you buy, cut them into fairly large slices to make turning them easy for you and serving them easy for the guest.**

     When the biscuits are baked, the oven is hot – raise the heat to broil. Follow the directions in the recipe for roasting the vegetables. This dish can be kept warm or served at room temperature.

- ◆ **When the vegetables are done, turn the heat down to 350°F and prepare the chickens as described in the recipe. Put them in the oven by 4PM. Prep cheese doodles but don't put cheese mix on bread yet.**
- ◆ **Make the cranberry compote. While it is heating up, set the table. Put the compote in a nice bowl and place it on the sideboard.**
- ◆ **Whip the cream for the shortcake. Place in a pretty**

bowl and keep refrigerated.
- ◆ **Take a swim or shower.**

5:45   **Set up the bar. Put cheese doodles in oven.**

6:00   **The guests arrive and you have plenty of time to chat and have a drink.**

6:30   **Take the chickens out and place them on the carving board. Heat the platter.**
- ◆ **Make the gravy and rice.**
- ◆ **Pour the water and light the candles.**
- ◆ **Carve the chickens onto the warm platter. Have a big soup pot handy so that the bones can go into the pot for chicken stock.**
- ◆ **Put the gravy into a bowl or pitcher.**
- ◆ **Put the rice out.**

7:00   **Dinner is served!**

Saturday

I am an early riser and enjoy the quiet of an early morning. I make the coffee, heat the oven for the muffins, start the sausage over a low flame, mix the muffin batter, and let it stand for 15 minutes so it puffs up a little while I have a cup of coffee and watch the day dawn. By the time the guests drift down for breakfast, the sausages are cooked, the muffins are ready, the fruit is out, and the apples for the pies are sliced into a bowl and tossed with sugar, cinnamon, nutmeg, and lemon juice to sit until I bake the pies later. I transfer the piecrusts from the freezer to the refrigerator.

     If breakfast is scheduled for 8 AM, this is the timetable:

7:00   **Put the muffins in a 350°F oven. Put a dot of butter into each muffin cup and heat the muffin tin in the oven for 3 to 4 minutes. This gives the batter a "lift" before it starts to bake and brown.**
- ◆ **While the muffins are baking, set the table, put out the grapefruit, and pour the juice.**
- ◆ **Slice the apples for the pies into a large bowl as directed.**

7:30   **The muffins come out of the oven. Let them cool**

Scrambled Eggs

| 8 eggs | 2 tablespoons butter |
| 1/2 cup heavy cream | 1/4 cup grated cheese (Parmesan works well) |

❉ Whisk the eggs and cream together until thoroughly mixed.

❉ Heat the butter in a cast-iron skillet until it bubbles. Pour in the egg mixture and keep stirring and scraping with a spoon until it looks firm and cooked. Add the cheese and serve.

Serves 6

for 10 minutes before removing them to a plate or basket. Prepare the egg mixture.

7:45   Cook the eggs.

8:00   Breakfast is served.

After breakfast I assign sandwich making to a guest. Chicken sandwiches are good with some cranberry compote on them. We pack up our lunches, making sure to include water, fruit, and cookies. Then we are off for a day at the lakes, hiking, or exploring.

3:00   I will be home, even if the guests decide to stay outside.

- ◆ Preheat the oven to 350°F and make the apple pies according to the recipe.
- ◆ While the pies are baking, wash and cut the potatoes, and put them in a roasting pan for baking later.
- ◆ Soak the salmon in cold water.
- ◆ Prepare the poaching court bouillon.
- ◆ Whip up some cream for the pies and put in a glass bowl and refrigerate.
- ◆ Set the table.
- ◆ Take the pies out to cool.
- ◆ Get showered and dressed.

5:30   Make the Hollandaise. Allow no interruptions during this process or you can curdle the sauce. Put it into a nice bowl and leave it at room temperature.

- ◆ Assign a guest and spouse to help you set up the bar and appetizers.

6:00   Put the potatoes in the oven.

- ◆ Turn the poacher on to heat the court bouillon.
- ◆ Soak the asparagus in cold water.
- ◆ Greet the guests and have a drink.

6:30   Put salmon in the poacher and cook it for 25 minutes.

6:45   Pour the water off of the asparagus and microwave as directed in the recipe.

- ◆ Warm the platter for the salmon.
- ◆ Light the candles and pour the water.
- ◆ Ask a spouse or guest to open the wine.

7:00   Transfer the salmon to the platter. Drizzle Hollandaise sauce over the top and sprinkle with chopped chives or fresh dill.

- ◆ Transfer the potatoes to a serving dish.

7:05   Dinner is served!

Hopefully you have someone to clean up. I love to cook but happily surrender the kitchen once dinner is on the table.

Sunday

7:00   Slice the bread for the French toast and prepare the egg mixture according to the recipe.

- ◆ Put the bacon on low heat.
- ◆ While the bacon cooks, make the salmon mousse and refrigerate it.
- ◆ Make the chicken salad and refrigerate it.
- ◆ Wash the lettuce and refrigerate it wrapped in a dish towel.
- ◆ Go to church or play golf or take a short hike after breakfast.

1:00   Set the table.

- ◆ Unmold the mousse.
- ◆ Toss the salad.

French Toast

12 slices French bread (or any dense bread)	1 teaspoon cinnamon
	1 teaspoon vanilla
6 eggs	Dash of nutmeg
1/2 cup milk	3 tablespoons butter

❉ Put the bread into a large lasagna dish.

❉ Beat the eggs and milk together and add the cinnamon, vanilla, and nutmeg.

❉ Pour the egg mixture over the bread. Let it soak in for 10 minutes. Turn the bread to soak the other side for 10 minutes.

❉ Melt 1 tablespoon butter on the griddle or in a skillet over medium heat. Cook 4 bread slices until browned on both sides. Repeat with remaining butter and bread.

❉ Serve with more butter and maple syrup.

Serves 6

◆ Prepare the cheese platter.

◆ Put the rolls or bread in a basket.

◆ Put everything out on the sideboard and ring the bell or call the guests. Because the guests will be driving home, I serve lemonade with lunch.

3:00 Everyone is on the road so that they will have plenty of time to drive during daylight hours.

Going Camping

If your camp cooking is taking place in the great outdoors, the following information is for camping by boat or car to a wilderness lean-to or tent site with a fireplace. These are suggestions for delicious yet simple meals for a weekend camping trip. (Backpacking is another matter, because every ounce has to be carried as well as the cooking pans and stove. All food must be freeze-dried and lightweight and can be purchased at a mountaineering shop.)

MENU

ARRIVAL DINNER

Steak

Potatoes, onions, and apples sautéed in butter, salt, and pepper

Fruit and cookies or s'mores

Wine and lemonade

BREAKFAST DAY 1

Coffee, tea, cocoa

Bacon – Cook a whole pound so you can make BLTs for lunch

Toasted bread on a stick: bring butter and small jar of jam

Fruit – oranges

LUNCH

BLTs – bring mayonnaise

Lemonade

Oranges and cookies

DINNER

Spaghetti with vegetables, oil, and garlic

Cake and fruit – kiwi?

Wine and lemonade

BREAKFAST DAY 2

Coffee, tea, cocoa

Oatmeal, raisins, nuts, and syrup

LUNCH EN ROUTE OUT

Ham and cheese sandwiches

Apples and cookies

EQUIPMENT LIST

Large skillet

A large pot to boil water

Cooler for the milk, butter, meats, vegetables

The day's newspaper to start the fire

Matches

Flashlight – a headlamp is great for seeing while you're cooking

Toilet paper if there is no outhouse

A shovel, if you need to dig a latrine

Tin foil for the sandwiches

Water bottles for the day trips

Small packs for day trips

Sleeping bags, towels

Cutting board, sharp knife

Dishes, pie plates are great

Forks & spoons & knives

Cups for hot drinks

Six *1* Complete Dinners

If you don't cook often or haven't ever cooked, the first thing to learn or relearn is *timing*. Anyone can read and execute a recipe, but when the roast is in the oven, have you planned to synchronize the rest of the meal?

As a young bride with no childhood experience cooking, the timing was the factor that tripped me up. My vegetables and potatoes would be done an hour before the roast was supposed to come out of the oven – or I would have it all ready and realize that I hadn't done the dessert yet. So for each of the six dinners in this chapter, I give a timetable so you can coordinate the various dishes. I hate to waste good leftovers so I've made a point to develop and collect recipes that can use the food that you don't eat for dinner. For each meal there's a list of possibilities for leftovers, and you'll find the recipes throughout the book.

Remember that this is camp cooking, so these dinners do not include appetizers, soup, or salad. Dessert suggestions are part of each menu, but often it is healthier and easier to serve fruit and cookies. A good camp meal is simply a main course, potatoes, vegetables, and dessert. Of course over the years we have come to expect more than nuts to accompany the cocktails. We expect at least a tossed baby greens salad (and perhaps cheese) after the main course. These are additions that have crept into our menus from our city lives and are not traditional camp cooking. Go ahead and add them if you like – there are chapters for starters and salads as well.

Kenneth's Meat Loaf Dinner

Meat Loaf

Green Beans

Mashed Potatoes

Kenneth's Apple Crisp

Here's Kenneth's (see box page 78) meat loaf dinner, my favorite meal Friday night when we would arrive from New York City. That is still my favorite time to serve it. The mashed potatoes go so well with meat loaf, the beans are easy to cook, and the apple crisp is a welcome treat after a long drive.

TIMING

The meat loaf will cook for two hours and does not have to sit like a roast before carving, so put it in the oven at 5PM for a 7PM dinner. Then make the potatoes and keep them warm. Prepare the apple crisp and put it into the oven when the meat loaf comes out. Cook the beans just before serving.

LEFTOVERS

Spaghetti & Meatballs (page 137)

Meat Loaf Sandwiches

Meat Loaf

Nothing could be easier to make than this meat loaf. And meat loaf sandwiches are always a big hit the next day.

2 pounds ground beef (the better the beef, the better the loaf)

1 large onion, chopped

2 cloves garlic, chopped

1/4 cup breadcrumbs

1 egg

Salt and pepper

1/4 teaspoon curry powder (optional–I added this later)

One 8-ounce can sliced tomatoes, drained

❈ Preheat the oven to 350°F.

❈ In a large bowl, mix all the ingredients except the tomatoes together with your hands. Form the mixture into a ball and throw it hard into a wooden bowl until all the meat becomes very smooth and sticks together. You probably have to throw it five times.

❈ Place the ball in a 4 x 9-inch loaf pan and shape it to fit. Top with the tomatoes.

❈ Bake for 2 hours. It will look like a well-done hamburger when done. Remove from the loaf pan and serve it on a platter.

Serves 6

Green Beans

If you do not have a microwave, sauté the beans in a cast-iron skillet with the butter, covered, for 5 to 7 minutes.

2 pounds green beans

2 tablespoons butter

Salt and pepper

❈ Cut or snap off the stem end of the beans. Soak them in cold water for 5 minutes.

❈ Drain the water off and place them in a glass microwave-proof bowl, cover with plastic wrap, and microwave for 5 minutes.

❈ Add the butter and toss them around with salt and pepper to taste. Serve immediately.

Serves 6

Kenneth Lawrence

Kenneth Lawrence was the son of Dana Lawrence, the caretaker of The Uplands. Dana was an outdoor man, tending the extensive vegetable garden in front of his cabin, and the flower garden in front of the main house. He mowed and cleaned the grounds, and cut blocks of ice from the pond in winter for use in next summer's "cooler." In 1924, he built his own cabin by the vegetable garden, and in 1936, he helped Uncle Peter build his little cabin by the flower garden.

Kenneth came back after World War II and a stint on Broadway as an actor, and fell into Dana's job as Dana aged and Kenneth needed something to do. My grandfather died in 1963 and Kenneth was the full-time caretaker living in Dana's cabin. Kenneth was an inside man: he preferred to cook rather than chop wood. He did a good job with the flowers but the vegetable garden went to grass and wildflowers.

All through my college years, Kenneth was the virtual chaperone for my fall and winter house parties. We used the servant's quarters, which had a coal furnace then and someone had to get up at 2 AM and shovel coal or the pipes would freeze. Kenneth did all the other shifts. He would arrive at 5 AM and stoke the furnace and build fires in the cookstove in the kitchen and the box stove in the dining room. He'd make coffee, oatmeal, and muffins and cook a pound of bacon. Then he would wait for us to get up. By the time we came in for breakfast, the room was as hot as a sauna.

After a day skiing or hiking, we'd come back to

Sure . . . he could cook!

a delicious camp dinner and a warm house with all the fires blazing. Meals were simple but tasty. Meat was cooked well-done, never rare; vegetables were cooked to death, never crunchy. But Kenneth had a magic touch with mashed potatoes — smooth and rich, gravy-thick, and delicious. He used only salt and pepper for spices and always lots of butter and heavy cream.

His jokes and stories amused us. Laughter encouraged relaxation and the flow of digestive juices.

Mashed Potatoes

I watched Kenneth make mashed potatoes once; he used Potato Buds from a box! I was shocked, but the potatoes were delicious because he used so much butter and cream. So this is my recipe.

Use one Idaho potato per person. This recipe is for six to eight tennis-ball-sized potatoes. You can also use Long Island potatoes or Iowa potatoes, but adjust the cooking time a little, as they have more starch and less fiber so they collapse into mashed potatoes faster.

1 potato per person
1 cup milk
2 cloves garlic, minced
8 tablespoons (1 stick) butter
1/2 cup cream
Salt and pepper

❋ Peel the potatoes and cut them into 1-inch chunks.

❋ Cover with water in a 3-quart pan, bring to a boil, and boil for 20 minutes.

❋ Drain. Add the milk and garlic. Cover the pot and simmer for 15 minutes.

❋ Add the butter and mash with a potato masher. Add salt and pepper to taste. Add the cream until the potatoes have the desired consistency.

❋ Serve in a warm bowl. They will get thicker as they sit around.

Serves 6

Kenneth's Apple Crisp

This is like an apple pie without the crust but has a topping made of sugar, butter, and flour. Kenneth made this often, so I renamed it Kenneth's apple crisp.

FOR THE FILLING

4 medium-size apples, sliced

3/4 cup brown sugar

1/4 cup chopped walnuts or pecans

2 tablespoons lemon juice

1/2 cup raisins

FOR THE TOPPING

8 tablespoons (1 stick) butter, softened

1/2 cup flour

3/4 cup brown sugar

1/4 teaspoon salt

❋ Preheat the oven to 350°F.

❋ Mix the filling ingredients together. Transfer to an oven-proof dish for baking.

❋ Mix the topping ingredients together in a small bowl using a wooden spoon. You have to press the sugar and flour into the butter. Distribute the topping evenly over the filling.

❋ Bake for 1 hour.

❋ Serve with heavy cream or ice cream.

Serves 6

Chicken Dinner

Roast Chicken with Pan Gravy

Cranberry Compote

Rice

Broccoli

Strawberry Shortcake

This is a meal that I often serve during a house party weekend; it is quintessential comfort food and yields plenty of leftover chicken for sandwiches for a trip to the lakes or a hike, and chicken salad for lunch on Sunday. I make the strawberry shortcake during strawberry season – generally late June through July.

TIMING

The chickens will roast for 2 to $2\frac{1}{2}$ hours so put them in first. Make the cranberry compote and set it aside. You can serve it warm or cool. Make the biscuits and slice the strawberries into a bowl. Whip the cream and refrigerate. The rice, broccoli, and gravy will all be made when the chickens come out of the oven and are sitting for 20 minutes before being carved.

LEFTOVERS

Basic Chicken Stock (page 110)
Cream of Broccoli Soup (page 111)
Chicken Pot Pie (page 158)
Chicken Salad (page 159)
Chicken Hash (page 159)

Cranberry Compote

In the fall I buy a lot of bags of cranberries and freeze them because sometimes they are hard to find in the spring and summer. The compote will keep in a large glass-lidded jar in the refrigerator all summer.

I bag fresh cranberries

1/2 cup sugar

1/4 cup orange juice

Zest of I orange (slivers)

I teaspoon cinnamon

Pinch of nutmeg

❄ Rinse the cranberries and place in a saucepan with high sides so it doesn't boil over. Add the sugar, juice, orange rind, cinnamon, and nutmeg. Bring to a boil. Lower the heat and simmer for 30 minutes or until the cranberries begin to pop.

❄ Transfer to a bowl and serve warm or cold.

Serves 6–8

Roast Chicken

I roast two chickens a week not only because chicken is so yummy, but then I have bones to make soup. Buy two small fryers instead of a large roasting hen, which is full of fat. Fryers are young and more tender and tastier. For soup, I put the bones in a large pot of water immediately after carving, throw in some chopped onions, carrots, and celery and leave on very low heat on the back of the stove overnight to draw the marrow out of the bones.

Two 4-pound fryers

1 head of garlic

1 ½ cups water

Salt and pepper

2 tablespoons Old Bay seasoning

2 sprigs of rosemary or thyme

❄ Preheat the oven to 350°F.

❄ Rinse the chickens inside and out. Pat dry with paper towels. Put them in a large roasting pan with 1 inch of water – this keeps the juices from burning and starts good gravy.

❄ Put the garlic in the pan. Season the chickens with salt and pepper and the Old Bay seasoning. Place a sprig of rosemary on top of each bird.

❄ Roast on the middle shelf of the oven for 1½ to 2 hours. The birds are done when golden brown and the drumstick moves easily side to side. You can test doneness by sticking a sharp knife in the breast; if the juices run clear, it's done.

❄ Transfer the birds to a platter and make the gravy.

Serves 6–8

Pan Gravy

Kenneth taught me how to make gravy. His only special ingredient was Gravy Master, which you can still find in some stores. I use soy sauce instead. It adds color and saltiness.

Cooked garlic cloves from the roasting pan

2 tablespoons fat from the roasting pan

2 tablespoons flour

1 cup water

1 cup pan juices

1 tablespoon soy sauce

Pepper

1 teaspoon dried rosemary or thyme

❈ Transfer the cooked garlic from the roasting pan to a cutting board and set aside. Pour the pan juices into a saucepan. Put the roasting pan on top of the stove over medium heat. Spoon two tablespoons of fat from the juices (it has floated to the top by now) into the roasting pan. If it's cooled, let it get hot, then whisk in the flour to make a roux.

❈ Add the water and whisk it around so the balls of roux dissolve.

❈ Skim the remaining fat from the pan juices with a large spoon. Add the juices to the roux mixture and whisk until smooth. Simmer for 3 or 4 minutes until it thickens.

❈ Add the soy sauce for color, and salt and pepper to taste. Add the same herb you used on the chicken – rosemary or thyme.

❈ Cut the bottom off the roasted garlic head, then cut in half horizontally. Lay each half on the cutting board and press down hard with the flat side of a large chopping knife. The roasted cloves will pop or ooze out. Chop them a bit and add to the gravy.

❈ Transfer to a gravy boat for serving.

Serves 6–8

Rice

I learned this rice recipe while taking Chinese cooking lessons. It's always perfect rice. The rice will be sticky (good for eating with chopsticks) unless you add the butter. If making larger or smaller batches, figure on ½ cup raw rice per person.

3 to 4 cups long-grain rice

❋ Place the rice in a saucepan with enough cold water to cover the rice by 1 inch (to the depth of a finger joint). Bring to a boil over medium heat.

❋ Boil until the water level drops to the rice and you see little craters. Turn off the heat and cover. Wait 10 minutes. Fluff with a fork and add butter.

Serves 6–8

Broccoli

For some reason, broccoli is the ideal vegetable to have with chicken.

I bunch broccoli

❋ Cut the heads off a bunch of broccoli and soak in cold water for 5 minutes (save the stems for soup).

❋ Drain the broccoli and place it in a microwave dish. Cover with plastic wrap and microwave for 7 minutes.

❋ Serve with either Hollandaise sauce (page 94) or a small pitcher of melted butter and lemon juice.

Serves 4

Strawberry Shortcake

There's nothing like fresh strawberry shortcake when the berries are in season. You can make the biscuits ahead.

FOR THE BISCUITS

3 cups Bisquick

1 cup milk

1 teaspoon cinnamon

FOR THE STRAWBERRIES

2 pints strawberries

1/2 cup sugar

1 teaspoon cinnamon

FOR THE WHIPPED CREAM

1 pint heavy cream

1/2 cup sugar

1 teaspoon vanilla extract

❋ **To make the biscuits:** Preheat the oven to 450°F. Stir the Bisquick, milk, and cinnamon in a glass bowl until a soft dough forms. Transfer the dough onto a surface (marble, stone, or wood) dusted in dry Bisquick.

❋ Roll the dough out to about 1 inch thick with a rolling pin or by pressing with your hands. Using a 3-inch-diameter cookie cutter or wine glass, cut out 6 biscuits and place them on a cookie sheet.

❋ Bake for 8 to 10 minutes until they are golden brown. Cool.

❋ **To prepare the strawberries:** Slice the strawberries into a glass bowl. Sprinkle with the sugar and cinnamon and refrigerate. (You can leave them at room temperature for 3 hours but they are better chilled.)

❋ **To prepare the whipped cream:** Whip the cream with a mixer or whisk, folding the sugar and vanilla extract in a little bit at a time. When the cream forms soft peaks, it is ready. It is best to whip the cream right before serving, but if you must do it ahead, refrigerate it in a bowl covered with plastic wrap.

❋ **To serve:** Cut the biscuits in half. Spoon strawberries onto each half and top with whipped cream.

Hint: With the leftover dough, you can add an egg, a bit more milk, mix and have pancakes the next morning!

Serves 6

Roast Beef Dinner

Roast Beef with Gravy and
Yorkshire Pudding
Pan-Roasted Potatoes
Zucchini & Onion Sauté
Berry Cobbler

This meal is a classic Sunday lunch after church, but I like to serve it for dinner. To me, Yorkshire pudding is true camp cooking because it is simple and delicious, yet spectacular. Berry cobbler for dessert offers a refreshing, juicy lift after a substantial meal. This menu allows you to serve an elegant and yummy meal with very little effort.

TIMING

Prepare the cobbler but don't bake it until the Yorkshire pudding is out of the oven. The roast will cook for 1 hour if it is boneless so it goes in first. The potatoes will cook for 45 minutes. If you use the same oven as the beef, add 15 minutes to the overall cooking time. When the beef comes out, make the Yorkshire pudding. While it is cooking for 20 minutes, do the gravy and zucchini. Put the cobbler in when the pudding comes out.

LEFTOVERS
Beef Stroganoff (page 166)
Roast Beef Hash (page 167)
Hungarian Goulash (page 170)

Roast Beef

You can buy a standing rib roast (with the bones in it) but it takes longer to cook; however, it also makes the best gravy. A rolled roast (bones removed) is what I usually get.

4- to 5-pound rolled rib roast

Salt and pepper

Leaves from 4 sprigs fresh thyme
or 1 tablespoon dried

1 cup water

1 head of garlic

❋ Preheat the oven to 350°F.

❋ Wash the roast and pat it dry with a paper towel. Place it in a roasting pan. Season it with salt, pepper, and thyme. Add 1/4 inch of water to the pan so the drippings don't burn. Put the garlic in the pan.

❋ If the roast is 4 inches in diameter, roast the meat for 1 hour; add 15 minutes per inch if it's larger. A standing rib will cook 15 minutes per pound. Transfer the roast to a carving board and let it rest while you make the gravy and Yorkshire pudding.

Serves 6–8

The dining room moose dressed for a wedding dinner

Yorkshire Pudding

This is the same recipe as popovers. You can make it in the roasting pan or a muffin tin. The trick is to have the pan HOT when you put the batter in it, and have the oven hot as well.

1 cup flour

3 eggs

1 cup milk

2 tablespoons melted butter or fat from the roasting pan

❋ Preheat the oven to 400°F.

❋ If you use the roasting pan, transfer the pan drippings to a saucepan or skillet and skim the fat off, putting 2 tablespoons of fat back in the roasting pan and saving some for the gravy. If you use a muffin tin, put a little fat or a dot of butter in each cup. Put the pan in the hot oven and heat the pan.

❋ Beat the flour, eggs, and milk together in a bowl. Pour the batter into the prepared hot pan.

❋ Bake for 20 minutes.

❋ If using the roasting pan, the pudding will bake like a soufflé, but since it is flat, it will look uneven. Serve by cutting into large squares.

❋ If using a muffin tin or popover pan serve right away! It's like a soufflé and will collapse as it cools.

Serves 6–8

Pan Gravy

Kenneth always used Gravy Master to darken the gravy and give it zest. I think soy sauce works just as well and is healthier. If you used the roasting pan for the Yorkshire pudding, use a cast-iron skillet for the gravy.

2 tablespoons fat from the roast

2 tablespoons flour

2 cups water

Pan drippings from roast

Salt and pepper

I tablespoon soy sauce

Leaves of I sprig thyme or rosemary (or I teaspoon dried)

❋ Combine the fat and flour in the skillet or roasting pan over medium heat and whisk it as it forms balls to make a roux. Whisk in the water and the pan drippings. Add the salt, pepper, and soy sauce. Add the thyme or rosemary. Simmer until it thickens into gravy.

Serves 6–8

Mock Gravy

If you don't have pan juices, or the bottom of the pan is burned, don't panic, you can make mock gravy!

I tablespoon butter

I tablespoon flour

I cup water

I beef bouillon cube

I tablespoon soy sauce

❋ Melt the butter in a saucepan over medium heat. Add the flour and whisk until it balls up. Add the water and bouillon cube and whisk until smooth. Add the soy sauce. Let it bubble until thick like gravy.

Makes about 1¼ cups

Pan-Roasted Potatoes

Once I had six Idaho potatoes to bake and noticed a couple of ugly spots. I cut the spots off, then cut the potatoes into finger-length strips and roasted them. They look and taste like giant healthy French fries. Plan on one potato per person.

2 tablespoons olive oil to oil the pan

6 Idaho potatoes

Salt and pepper

❄ Preheat the oven to 350°F. Oil a shallow baking pan.

❄ Peel and cut the potatoes into finger-size pieces. Place the chunks on the prepared pan. Season the potatoes with salt and pepper.

❄ Bake for 45 minutes or until the potatoes are golden. If you use the same oven as the roast beef, add 10 minutes to the cooking time.

Serves 6

Zucchini & Onion Sauté

This is particularly delicious in August when zucchini ripens in Adirondack gardens.

3 tablespoons butter

3 zucchini, cut into 1/4-inch-thick slices

1 onion, sliced

Salt and pepper

1 tablespoon fresh dill

❄ Melt the butter in a skillet over medium heat. Add the zucchini and onion and sauté until the zucchini is hot but still crunchy (about 8 minutes).

❄ Add salt and pepper to taste and the dill.

Serves 6–8

Berry Cobbler

You can use blueberries, raspberries, peaches, or plums. For the topping you can use either piecrust or short-cake biscuit dough (see page 85). Hopefully you have piecrusts in the freezer. The piecrust is preferred as it is flakier but biscuit dough works well too.

4 cups fresh berries

1½ cups sugar

3 tablespoons flour

1 tablespoon cinnamon

1/4 teaspoon nutmeg

3 tablespoons lemon juice

1 tablespoon grated lemon zest

2 teaspoons butter, cut into small pieces

One 10-inch piecrust or 1 recipe shortcake biscuit dough

(see Strawberry Shortcake recipe)

❄ Preheat the oven to 350°F.

❄ In a large bowl, combine the washed berries, the sugar, flour, cinnamon, nutmeg, and lemon zest and juice and stir well.

❄ Transfer the mixture to an ovenproof baking dish. Top with the butter and then the piecrust or biscuit dough.

❄ Bake for 45 minutes or until the top is browned and the filling is bubbling.

❄ Serve with whipped cream, heavy cream, or ice cream.

Serves 6

Salmon Dinner

Poached Salmon with Hollandaise Sauce
Asparagus
Rice (page 84)
Chocolate Bread Pudding

Wild salmon is delicious either grilled or poached. However, it is not always readily available. Farmed salmon is available year-round but is not as tasty and is, I'm told, higher in fat and cholesterol. Still, it makes a good dinner if poached in court bouillon and served with Hollandaise.

The court bouillon gives it flavor and removes any fishy smell. Hollandaise is good on many things but especially on salmon and asparagus, so why not serve them together? A simple chocolate dessert makes a perfect ending to this tasty meal.

TIMING
You can prepare the bread pudding in advance and bake it while you are eating the main course. Make the court bouillon and Hollandaise ahead. Poach the fish and make the rice at the same time. The asparagus takes only 15 minutes and can be started just before you transfer the fish to a warm platter.

LEFTOVERS
Salmon Mousse (page 188)
Rice Pudding (page 213)

Asparagus

Fresh asparagus shares the same season as salmon, and it goes so well with the Hollandaise. A double recipe of Hollandaise is enough for both the salmon and the asparagus.

2 bunches asparagus

❋ Cut the white ends off the bunch of asparagus and soak the green asparagus in cold water for 15 minutes. Drain off the water and cover with plastic wrap and microwave for 6 minutes.

❋ If you don't have a microwave, sauté the asparagus in 2 tablespoons butter in a sauté pan or the cast-iron skillet for 6 minutes.

Serve 6–8

Poached Salmon with Hollandaise Sauce

Wild salmon fight their way from the ocean upstream to spawn in the spring. If they are caught during this period, the meat is full of nutrients, and tasty. Salmon don't eat when they are swimming upstream to spawn; hence the longer the river, the more densely packed the nutrients are likely to be in the flesh.

Two of the tastiest types of salmon are Copper River Kings (Chinook) and Yukon River White Kings (Chinook as well), as these rivers are exceptionally long and produce superior fish.

If you have no poacher, use a roasting pan and tie the fish into cheesecloth. This will make it easier to lift the salmon out onto a platter.

FOR THE COURT BOUILLON

2 cups water

2 cups white wine or champagne

I onion, chopped

1/2 bunch parsley

Thyme or dill – I tablespoon dried or leaves from 2 sprigs fresh

Salt and pepper

FOR THE FISH

I side fresh salmon, approximately 3½ to 4 pounds

Hollandaise Sauce (page 94)

Chopped dill, for garnish

❋ **To make the court bouillon:** Combine the court bouillon ingredients in the poacher, and bring to a boil. Lower the heat to medium, and boil for 10 minutes.

❋ **To prepare the salmon:** Soak the salmon in cold water for 30 minutes to remove any fishy smell.

❋ When you are ready to poach the salmon, place it on the poacher rack. Cover and poach (simmer) for 20–25 minutes. To check for doneness, insert a sharp knife and peek inside – the salmon is done when it is flaky.

❋ Transfer the fish to a warm platter.

❋ If using the poacher, slide the fish off the strainer insert.

❋ If using the roasting pan, lift the fish out holding the ends of the cheesecloth and place it on the platter; then carefully pull the cheesecloth off.

❋ **To serve:** Put a few spoons full of Hollandaise (recipe follows on next page) top, and garnish with chopped dill.

Serves 6–8

Hollandaise Sauce

This rich and creamy sauce is not difficult, but it takes advance organization and complete focus on the pot once you start. Make Hollandaise ahead while it's quiet; do not answer the phone, let the dog in, or greet guests. Hollandaise can sit at room temperature during cocktails. It will go on hot food and that will heat it up. DO NOT TRY TO REHEAT IT *or it will curdle.*

1/4 cup white vinegar

8 tablespoons (1 stick) cold butter cut into 8 squares

3 very fresh eggs yolks (save the egg whites for scrambled eggs)

❊ Use a heavy saucepan and a wire whisk (do not use a double boiler). Have a cold, wet washcloth on the side of the stove to put the pot on in order to cool it off quickly.

❊ Put the vinegar in the saucepan and bring to a boil. Boil until it is reduced to just 1 tablespoon.

❊ Add 2 squares of the cold butter; as they melt, add the egg yolks and whisk like crazy.

❊ Whisk in the remaining butter, 1 square at a time, and take the pot off the stove as the butter melts and place it on the cool cloth to stop the cooking process. The sauce should be thick and smooth.

❊ Serve in a warm (but not too warm!) bowl.

Serves 4

Tips for Perfect Hollandaise

❊ Use very fresh eggs

❊ You do not want the egg to scramble. The butter will cool the egg. As the butter melts, the egg will cook SLOWLY. It's a fine balance. You want just enough heat to melt the butter and cook the egg.

❊ I add the butter off the heat, and if it won't melt, I put the pot back on the flame only long enough to see the butter starting to melt.

Chocolate Bread Pudding

I have always loved bread pudding but this one is with chocolate. I love it so much I serve it as my birthday cake! I first had is at a little family "roadside" restaurant somewhere outside of Boston. I asked the cook how she did it and she said "Oh I just soak the bread in Hershey Syrup first." So here is a terrific chocolate dessert.

This is a great way to use stale bread. In fact, do not use fresh bread. It can be whole wheat, white, or sourdough; do not use rye or pumpernickel etc.

3 cups of stale bread, broken into small bite-size pieces, crusts and all

One 10-ounce can chocolate syrup

1½ cups milk

1 cup heavy cream

3 eggs

1/4 cup sugar

1/4 teaspoon vanilla extract

1/2 cup chocolate chips

1 teaspoon cinnamon

1/4 teaspoon nutmeg

1 cup slivered almonds for the top

❋ Put the bread pieces into a 7 x 9-inch lasagna-type baking dish. Pour the chocolate syrup over the bread and cover with plastic wrap and leave it for an hour or all day.

❋ In a bowl, beat together the milk, cream, eggs, sugar, and vanilla. Pour this mixture over the bread. Stir in the chocolate chips.

❋ Sprinkle the cinnamon and nutmeg on top and distribute the almonds over the top. Press down with your hands to be sure all the bread is saturated. Let it sit for 15 to 20 minutes before baking.

❋ Preheat the oven to 350°F.

❋ Bake for 1 hour or until firm when touched in the middle. Serve warm with heavy cream.

Serves 6

Lamb Dinner

Roast Leg of Lamb with Pan Gravy

Baked Apples & Cranberries

Mashed Potatoes (page 79)

Peas

Mock Tiramisu

Roast lamb seems special, and is a nice change from roast beef and chicken. I like to serve this meal on a cool spring or crisp fall night. The apples with cranberries and the peas make for a very pretty plate. A light but "melt-in-your-mouth" dessert of mock tiramisu is a grand finale.

TIMING

Make the dessert a day ahead if possible. If the lamb is to be served at 7 PM, with cocktails at 6 PM, you should have it in the oven by 4:30 PM. You can do the mashed potatoes ahead and keep them warm, so I would do them after the roast goes in the oven. Then prepare the apples; they will go in the oven when the roast comes out at 6:30 and while you are making gravy and heating the peas. The lamb can be carved at 6:50. Everything will be ready for dinner at 7 o'clock.

LEFTOVERS

Shepard's Pie (page 174)

Potato Pancakes (page 148)

Lamb Curry (page 176)

Moussaka (page 175)

Baked Apples & Cranberries

This is an apple recipe, but it is a good garnish for lamb when apples are in season and look pretty on the platter. If you have only one oven, bake the apples first and just keep them warm or serve at room temperature.

8 apples

8 teaspoons brown sugar

48 fresh or dried cranberries

Cinnamon

8 teaspoons butter

❉ Preheat the oven to 350°F. Line a baking dish with tin foil.

❉ Core the apples by taking a small sharp paring knife and digging around the stem at an angle about 2 inches deep (don't go through the other side!) Discard the core and top of the stem.

❉ Fill the hole in each apple with: 6 cranberries, 1 teaspoon brown sugar, and a dash of cinnamon. Top each apple with a teaspoon of butter.

❉ Bake the apples for 35 to 40 minutes.

Serves 8

Roast Leg of Lamb

I remember eating lots of lamb as a child and it certainly was a regular meal at The Uplands. However, recently I have found it harder to find lamb, and when I do it is very expensive if locally raised. The most affordable lamb comes from Australia and New Zealand and is often frozen and then thawed. It is tender and delicious but generally smaller so you won't have as many leftovers for shepard's pie if you invite 10 people for the roast lamb dinner. Pan gravy is the same method no matter what you roast: chicken, lamb, or beef.

8- to 10-pound leg of lamb (bone in)

1 head of garlic

1½ cups water

Salt and pepper

1 sprig rosemary

Pan Gravy (page 97)

❀ Preheat the oven to 350°F.

❀ Wash and dry the lamb. Place it in a roasting pan with 1 inch of water to catch the drippings and prevent burning (this also gives you a head start on the gravy).

❀ Put the garlic in the pan. Salt and pepper the roast, and place a sprig of rosemary on top.

❀ Roast the lamb for 2 hours or until a knife goes in easily.

❀ Transfer the roast to a warm platter while you make the gravy.

Serves 8–10

Peas

You have spent a lot of time doing the garnish, so do a simple vegetable. Of course fresh peas are best, but you don't see them often. Frozen peas will taste like fresh if you don't overcook them.

4 boxes frozen peas, thawed

4 tablespoons butter

❀ Place the peas in a cast-iron skillet with the butter and heat them until hot, about 5 to 6 minutes.

Serves 8

Mock Tiramisu

My mother made this up, although she really could not cook. This is delicious and it's so easy. All of our guests love it. Make it a day ahead if possible – it will taste much better and have a better texture. This recipe makes six generous servings; make two for a hungry crowd.

2 envelopes Knox gelatin

2 cups leftover coffee, heated

2½ cups heavy cream

6 tablespoons sugar

1 cup sour cream

1 teaspoon vanilla extract

1 Sara Lee pound cake

1 square unsweetened Bakers chocolate, grated

❄ In a small bowl, soften the gelatin in 2 tablespoons of cool water. Add the hot coffee and stir until the gelatin is melted. Add 1/2 cup of the cream and 4 tablespoons of the sugar.

❄ Whip the remaining 2 cups of cream to stiff peaks.

❄ In a separate bowl, stir together 1 cup of the whipped cream, the sour cream, the remaining 2 tablespoons sugar, and the vanilla. Refrigerate the remaining whipped cream.

❄ Take out a glass lasagna dish. Cut the pound cake into 3 lengthwise slices. Place one slice in the dish and pour one-third of the coffee mix over it slowly so it soaks in. Spoon half of the whipped cream–sour cream mixture on top.

❄ Top with another slice of pound cake, one-third of the coffee mixture, and the rest of the whipped cream–sour cream mixture. Repeat with the last slice of pound cake and the remaining coffee mixture. Cover with plastic wrap and refrigerate for 3 hours.

❄ To serve, cover the whole cake with the reserved whipped cream. (I like to take the cake out of the dish and put it on a platter with the coffee Jello like foam all around it.)

❄ Sprinkle grated chocolate on top.

Serves 6

Variation: I like this even better – alternating slices of pound cake and stale chocolate cake. Do not use moist, fresh chocolate cake or it will fall apart.

Ham Dinner

Baked Ham with Honey Mustard
Three-Potato Pie
Sautéed Pineapple Rings
Sautéed Red Pepper Slices
Tarte Tatin

I love to serve this hearty, tasty meal when we get our first cold nights at the end of August. Everyone is delighted to see a large platter of sliced ham rimmed with sautéed pineapple rings and a dish of bubbling potato pie next to it. The apple dessert is a sure sign that fall is in the air.

TIMING
Both the potato pie and the tart can be assembled in advance. The ham will bake for 15 to 30 minutes per pound at 325°F depending on how much it is smoked and precooked, so the ham will go in first. Follow the directions on the ham package. After cooking, the ham can stay out in a warm spot – on top of the stove – while the potatoes are cooking. Put the tart in the oven before you sit down to dinner. Do the pineapple rings and red pepper slices just before serving. Honey-mustard can be made at any time and kept refrigerated all summer.

LEFTOVERS
Split Pea Soup (page 113)
Skillet Corn Bread (page 126)
Ham Hash (page 180)
Eggs Benedict (page 180)

Baked Ham

A cooked ham will last a long time unless you are cooking for 20. Half a ham will be plenty of meat for 8–10 people. I like to buy a ham with the bone in so you can make pea soup later. Most hams come partially cooked and smoked. The glaze is totally unnecessary, but it makes the ham taste even better.

FOR THE HAM

Half ham

FOR THE GLAZE

1/2 cup molasses

1/4 cup brown sugar

1/4 cup Dijon mustard

FOR THE HONEY MUSTARD

One 4-ounce jar Dijon mustard

4 ounces honey

❋ Preheat the oven to 325°F.

❋ Line the bottom of a roasting pan with tin foil (or the ham juices and glaze will form a hard crust on the bottom that is almost impossible to clean). Wash the ham and place it in the pan. Bake according to directions on the ham package.

❋ While the ham is cooking, prepare the glaze. Stir the molasses, brown sugar, and mustard together. During the last hour, baste the ham with the glaze.

❋ For the honey mustard, stir together the honey and the mustard. (After dinner, store in a recycled jam or mayonnaise jar in the refrigerator.)

❋ Remove the ham from the oven and place on a board for carving. Arrange the slices on a warm platter. Put pineapple rings around the outside rim of the platter. Serve with the honey mustard.

Serves 8–10

Three-Potato Pie

While this takes time to assemble, it is worth it! You can prepare this in advance, bake it ahead, and keep it warm for hours. It is incredibly rich, savory, and creamy.

4 tablespoons (1/2 stick) butter

5 cloves garlic, 1 whole, 4 chopped

2 large white baking potatoes (Idaho potatoes are the best!)

2 large sweet potatoes

4 to 6 yellow (Yukon gold) or red potatoes

1 cup heavy cream

1 cup sour cream

Salt and pepper

❉ Preheat the oven to 350°F.

❉ Use a large glass baking dish that you would use for lasagna or brownies – 13 x 9 inches. Spread 1 tablespoon of the butter around the dish and rub the butter with a clove of garlic. Sprinkle the chopped garlic on the bottom of the dish.

❉ Peel all the potatoes and keep them in a bowl of cold water until you slice them.

❉ You will be layering the three types of potatoes, so start with the baking potatoes. Slice them very thin. Use a mandoline if you have it, otherwise use a VERY sharp knife and slice as thin as possible.

❉ Layer the slices in the pan and sprinkle with salt and pepper. Dot the potatoes with butter. Repeat the same procedure with the sweet potatoes, then the Yukon gold. Keep layering until you reach 1 inch from the top of the dish (usually 5 to 6 layers).

❉ Mix the cream and sour cream together and pour the mixture along the sides until it reaches the top of the potatoes. Put dots of butter on top.

❉ Bake for 45 to 60 minutes. It's done when a knife goes in easily and the top is golden. The potatoes will soak up most of the cream.

Serves 8–10

Sautéed Pineapple Rings

Pineapple and ham complement each other, and the pineapple looks pretty around the platter. Pineapple rings also make a great dessert. Add maple syrup during the last minute of cooking and serve with ice cream or whipped cream.

1 fresh pineapple

4 tablespoons butter

❊ Cut the ends off the pineapple. Then slice off the skin. Cut the pineapple into 1/2- to 3/4-inch-thick slices. Do not bother cutting the core out.

❊ Melt 1 tablespoon of the butter in a cast-iron skillet or on a griddle. When the the butter sizzles, sauté 4 pineapple slices at a time for 5 minutes a side. Repeat with the remaining butter and pineapple slices.

❊ Arrange the pineapple around the edge of the ham platter.

Serves 8–10

Sautéed Red Pepper Slices

2 tablespoons olive oil

4 cloves garlic, minced

4 red bell peppers cut into thin finger-long pieces

1 tablespoon chopped fresh basil

Salt and pepper

❊ Heat the oil in a cast-iron skillet over high heat. Add the garlic and cook for 2 minutes. Add the pepper slices and sauté them for 5 minutes, flipping frequently. Add the basil and salt and pepper to taste. The peppers should be hot but still crunchy. Serve in a warm dish.

Serves 8–10

Tarte Tatin

This recipe can also be made with bananas or pears, though the classic French dessert is usually made with apples. It is very easy to make and looks spectacular as well as being delicious. Plan on this coming out of the oven about an hour before the guests arrive. If you make it too early, the pastry will get soggy.

3 apples, peeled and cut into very thin, even slices

1 tablespoon lemon juice

1 teaspoon cinnamon

1/4 teaspoon nutmeg

1/2 cup sugar

1 tablespoon water

2 tablespoons butter

1 sheet puff pastry

❋ Preheat the oven to 350°F.

❋ In a frying pan or cast-iron skillet, heat the sugar with the water. Let it boil until the sugar turns golden, about 5 minutes. Immediately pour it into a pie dish. It will harden into a nice caramel but will melt later when you cook it with the apples.

❋ In a bowl, combine the apples, lemon juice, cinnamon, and nutmeg. Toss to coat all the slices.

❋ Arrange the apples on top of the cooled caramel by starting a fan in the center and overlapping the slices a little. When you serve the tart you will flip it upside down so the bottom is really the top, so it should look even and pretty. After the first pretty layer, just put the other slices on in any arrangement. Dot the top with butter.

❋ Place the puff pastry on top and cut the 4 corners off so it fits exactly the round shape of the pie dish.

❋ Bake for 35 to 40 minutes, until the pastry is golden.

❋ Immediately remove from the oven and place a large round plate over the top of the pie. Flip it so the pastry is now on the bottom and the pretty fan of apples is the top. Leave the pie plate upside down. You may have to wait 5 to 10 minutes for some apple slices to drop into place.

❋ Serve with whipped cream.

Serves 6–8

2 Appetizers & Soups

Camp cooking is traditionally meat, potatoes, vegetables, and dessert – no appetizers, salad, or soup. But I have found that guests like something to nibble on while having a cocktail, and sometimes soup is a good way to get everyone seated and eating while the main course (usually a grilled meat) is still cooking. Soups, of course, are also wonderful for lunch.

Appetizers

Soups

APPETIZERS

I hate to take time to make fussy, tiny hors d'oeuvres that disappear in seconds. I would rather spend the time on the main meal, but most people like something to nibble on with cocktails. Cheese doodles are my favorite. My other quick favorite is cucumber tea sandwiches made on bread rounds. I always have nuts and Greek olives on hand as well.

Cheese Doodles

These are not the bright orange snack food! This recipe came about after a house party weekend when I found six or seven small pieces of cheese left over from a large cheese platter. I grated all of the hard cheeses into a bowl, added onion and enough mayonnaise to hold it together, and spread it on a cracker. It needed cooking so I tried baking it on bread and it was so good! I use the simple, cheap white bread as I find it works better than whole wheat or other, more substantial bread. I've found that Brie, Camembert, and blue cheeses do not work, so it's best to stick to the hard cheeses.

Keep leftover mix in a tight container in the refrigerator and add to it at will. Keep a loaf of white bread in the freezer. It's great to have something on hand for the unexpected guest.

I pound grated cheeses, mozzarella, Parmesan, and/or cheddar

I small sweet onion, diced

About 1/2 cup mayonnaise

I loaf white bread

❋ Preheat the oven to 350°F.

❋ In a bowl mix the cheeses together. Stir in the onion and enough mayonnaise to hold everything together.

❋ Using a cookie cutter or small juice glass, cut the bread into rounds (4 per slice). Spread the cheese mixture onto the bread rounds.

❋ Bake for 15 minutes or until golden brown.

Serves 1 slice of bread/person so 1 loaf will serve 20

Hot Artichoke Dip

This recipe is enough for two soup bowls of dip. I keep one in the refrigerator for the inevitable unexpected cocktail party.

One 4-ounce jar artichoke hearts, drained

1/2 cup mayonnaise

1/2 cup grated Parmesan cheese

❋ Combine the artichokes, mayonnaise, and cheese in the blender or food processor and blend until smooth, about 2 minutes.

❋ Pour the mixture into a pretty ovenproof dish (or 2 small ones) and bake for 15 minutes. Serve hot with crackers or hearty bread broken into bite-size pieces.

Makes about 2 cups

Asparagus Tips in Phyllo Dough

1 bunch asparagus with 2 inches of tips cut off

4 sheets phyllo dough

2 tablespoons butter, softened

❋ Preheat the oven to 350°F.

❋ Rinse the cut asparagus tips, place them in a glass baking dish, cover with plastic wrap, and microwave on high for 7 minutes.

❋ Unroll the sheets of phyllo and cut into strips about 2 inches wide.

❋ Butter the dough strips and roll each asparagus tip in a phyllo strip so that the phyllo wraps around the asparagus twice.

❋ Place them on a cookie sheet and bake for 15 minutes or until the dough is golden brown.

❋ To serve, arrange on a round plate like spokes of a bicycle wheel. Serve hot or warm.

Serves 6–8

Red Pepper/Anchovy Rounds

When assembled, these anchovy rounds are very colorful. They taste like a wonderful Italian antipasto. In fact I have eaten roasted red peppers with anchovy as a first course in Italy.

4 slices bread

2 tablespoons butter

One 2-ounce can rolled anchovies with caper in each one

1 roasted red pepper, seeded and cut into large pieces

❋ Using a small cookie cutter or juice glass, cut rounds of bread out of the slices. Butter each round. Cut the red pepper into rounds with the cookie cutter. Put a round of red pepper on top of each round of buttered bread. Place a rolled anchovy on top.

Makes 12 small appetizers

Mushroom Sauté on Toast Rounds

These are quick, easy, and delicious – they make a great last-minute hot appetizer.

1/2 pound mushrooms (any combination or type), finely chopped

1 tablespoon butter

1 small onion, chopped

1 clove garlic, chopped

1 tablespoon heavy cream

Salt and pepper

2 tablespoons Cognac or Applejack (optional)

6 slices bread

❋ Sauté the chopped mushrooms in a little butter with the onions and garlic. When all the mushroom fluid is cooked out, add the cognac and let it boil off. Add the cream, and salt and pepper to taste. Continue cooking until the mixture thickens.

❋ Using a small cookie cutter or juice glass, cut rounds of bread out of the slices. Toast the rounds.

❋ Spread the warm mushroom mixture onto the toasted bread rounds and serve.

Makes 24 small appetizers

Tea Sandwiches

How often do we sit down and have afternoon tea poured from a pot and served with little tea sandwiches? Almost never! As a result, these delectable morsels have made a nice transition to the cocktail hour and are all made with common garden vegetables (except the watercress). They are so refreshing on a hot summer evening.

Cucumber Rounds

❄ Spread either butter or mayonnaise onto bread rounds. Slice a cucumber into thin rounds and place one slice on top of each bread round. Salt and pepper them. Add a tiny bit of fresh dill on top.

Radish Rounds

❄ Spread either butter or mayonnaise onto bread rounds. Place thin slices of radish on top. You will usually need 3 radish slices per round. Salt and pepper them.

Chevre, Pear, and Oregano Rounds

❄ Spread chevre (goat cheese) onto rounds of bread. Place thin slices of pear on top and then a piece of fresh oregano.

Watercress Sandwiches

❄ These will not work as a round or open-faced sandwich. For one sandwich butter two slices of fresh white bread and place a 5 or 6 sprigs of watercress on one of the slices. Top with the other slice. Place a clean dish towel on top and press down with your hand or a rolling pin to compress the sandwich. Cut off the crusts. Then cut into three long thin pieces or four square pieces.

SOUPS

These soups make for a wonderful lunch or a first course for dinner. Camp cooking is simple meals, but sometimes it is nice to have everyone seated and eating happily while the meat is grilling. Most of my soups start with a good chicken broth: so always save the bones from your roast chicken dinner. You can freeze them in a sealable freezer bag if you don't want to cook them immediately. I like to roast two chickens a week just so I will have stock ready for soups and sauces. You can freeze it in 8-ounce containers. If you don't have them, an empty coffee can works fine. Remember to label it – everything in the freezer looks alike. If you don't have your own stock in the freezer, use a good canned chicken broth or even chicken bouillon cubes (but it's always better with your own stock!).

Basic Chicken Stock

The following recipe is for the leftovers from two small fryers or one large (8-pound) roasting hen.

Bones from 2 small roasted fryers

1 onion, quartered

1 head of garlic (unpeeled) with the bottom stem cut off

Salt and pepper to taste

2 sprigs fresh rosemary or thyme, or 2 teaspoons dried

❈ Put the bones into a large stockpot and cover them with water. Add the remaining ingredients and bring to a boil. Simmer for 3 hours or all night. I leave my stockpot on the lowest flame for two days. Chicken bones have something healing in them and it takes time to cook out into the broth.

❈ Strain the broth into a bowl and refrigerate. The fat will float to the top and then it's easy to remove (I save it for the dogs).

❈ You can freeze the stock or use it immediately for soup or chicken pot pie.

Makes 1 quart

Cream of Broccoli Soup

This recipe can be used for a variety of vegetable cream soups – cream of broccoli soup, cream of mushroom soup, cream of cauliflower soup, and others. With vegetables that need a longer cooking time, precook them in the microwave for 5 minutes before you start the sauté process. I use broccoli stems for this soup, plus any leftover florets from the roast chicken dinner. You can use either a little nutmeg or cumin to make this soup more exotic. Do not use both! Ok to use olive oil instead of butter, if you prefer. Instead of chicken broth, you could use vegetable broth. Instead of half-and-half, use coconut milk or another plant-based milk.

Stems of large bunch broccoli, sliced (2 cups)

1 tablespoon butter or olive oil

1 medium onion, chopped

2 cups chicken stock

1 tablespoon fresh thyme or 1 teaspoon dried

1 cup half-and-half

Salt and pepper

1/4 teaspoon ground nutmeg or cumin (optional)

❋ Microwave the broccoli on high for 5 minutes.

❋ In a soup pot, melt the butter or warm the olive oil over medium heat. Add the onion and sauté for 2 minutes or until it is transparent. Add the chicken stock, broccoli, thyme, and salt and pepper to taste. Bring to a boil, reduce the heat and simmer for 45 minutes.

❋ Using a blender or food processor, combine 1/2 cup of the half-and-half with 1 cup of the broccoli mixture and whirl away until you have a nice cream soup, about 1 minute. Transfer the mixture to a large saucepan. Repeat with the remaining half-and-half and broccoli mixture. Reheat the soup and correct the seasoning as needed.

Serves 6

Cream of Tomato Soup

This is my favorite soup. My mother loved it and would say, "Oh, this is sooo good!" Ok to use olive oil instead of butter, if you prefer. Instead of chicken broth, you could use vegetable broth. Instead of cream, use half-and-half, or coconut milk, or another plant-based milk.

1 tablespoon butter

1 medium onion, chopped

6 tomatoes cut into small chunks to make 2 cups

1 tablespoon dried basil, oregano, dill, or thyme

2 cups chicken stock

1 cup heavy cream

Salt and pepper

❈ In a large soup pot, melt the butter and sauté the onion for 3 minutes. Stir in the tomatoes and herb of choice and cook over medium heat for 5 minutes. Add the chicken stock and simmer for 30 minutes.

❈ Using a blender or food processor, combine 1/2 cup of the cream with 1 cup of the tomato mixture and whirl away until you have a nice cream soup, about 1 minute. Transfer the mixture to a large saucepan. Repeat this process with the remaining cream and tomato mixture. Reheat the soup and correct the seasoning as needed.

Serves 6

Corn Chowder

This very satisfying soup is simplicity itself – real camp cooking!

3 slices bacon, cut into little bits

1 medium onion, chopped

2 cups chicken stock

2 cups corn kernels (fresh, frozen, or canned)

1 teaspoon dried thyme

1/4 teaspoon nutmeg

Salt and pepper

1 cup heavy cream

Chopped chives or scallion tops, for garnish

❈ In a heavy soup pot, sauté the bacon and onion until browned. Add the chicken stock, corn, thyme, nutmeg, and salt and pepper to taste. Simmer for 30 minutes.

❈ Stir in the cream and adjust the seasoning. Sprinkle with chopped chives or scallion tops before serving.

Serves 6

Oyster Stew

This is all you need for lunch after skiing fresh snow all morning. You can throw it together in 15 minutes if you have all the ingredients organized ahead of time.

10 tablespoons (I stick plus
2 tablespoons) butter

1/2 medium onion, chopped

2 stalks celery, chopped

I cup chicken stock

I can cream of mushroom soup

One 6-ounce can whole oysters

I teaspoon paprika

1/2 teaspoon pepper

1/4 teaspoon salt

1/2 teaspoon Old Bay seasoning

I cup heavy cream

❊ Drain the liquid from the oysters and set it aside.

❊ In a 3-quart saucepan melt 4 tablespoons of the butter. Add the onion and celery and sauté until they have softened, about 4 minutes.

❊ Add the chicken stock, mushroom soup, seasonings, and reserved oyster liquid. Simmer for 7 minutes.

❊ Add the cream and oysters and simmer for 5 minutes more.

❊ Pour into warm bowls and top each with a pat of butter.

Serves 6

Split Pea Soup

A hearty pea soup is easy to make, and tastes great after a day of hiking or skiing. Go ski or play golf! Serve the soup with Skillet Corn Bread (page 126).

I bag split dried peas

I ham bone

I large onion, chopped

6 carrots, peeled and sliced

6 cups water

I tablespoon fresh thyme leaves
or I teaspoon dried

Salt and pepper

❊ Rinse the peas in cold water and place in a large, heavy soup pot. Add the remaining ingredients. Bring to a boil, reduce the heat, and simmer for 3 to 4 hours.

❊ You can serve as is after removing the bone, or for a creamy pea soup you can combine the soup with 1 cup half-and-half (in batches as directed in all the cream soup recipes).

Serves 8–10

Cream of Squash Soup

This is a basic soup for any orange squash such as acorn, butternut, or pumpkin. Note that you need to pre-cook the squash, either baked whole or peeled, cut, and cooked in the microwave. You can also use this recipe for carrot soup, as explained in the next recipe. Ok to use olive oil instead of butter, if you prefer. Instead of chicken broth, you could use vegetable broth. Instead of cream, use half-and-half, or coconut milk, or another plant-based milk.

I squash (peeled and cut into pieces to measure 2 cups if microwaving)

I tablespoon butter or olive oil

2 small onions, chopped

2 cups chicken stock

I tablespoon fresh thyme or I teaspoon dried

Salt and pepper

I cup heavy cream

❄ Precook the squash in the microwave for 5 minutes or bake in the oven at 350°F for 45 minutes. If baking, scoop the squash out of the skin.

❄ Melt the butter or warm the olive oil in a soup pot. Add the onions and sauté until translucent. Add the squash, chicken stock, thyme, and salt and pepper to taste. Simmer for 30 minutes.

❄ Using a blender or food processor, combine 1/2 cup of the cream with 1 cup of the squash mixture and whirl away until you have a nice cream soup, about 1 minute. Transfer the mixture to a large saucepan. Repeat this process with the remaining cream and squash mixture. Reheat the soup and correct the seasoning as needed.

Serves 6

Cream of Carrot Soup

Use the same recipe as the squash soup above, but substitute 1 bunch of peeled, sliced carrots for the squash. Cook the carrots in the microwave for 5 minutes or boil in a cup of water for 5 minutes, then proceed with the recipe. Substitute 1 slice of chopped fresh ginger or 1 teaspoon ground ginger instead of thyme.

Curried Cream of Carrot Soup

This is a terrific soup to serve cold in the summer and hot in cooler temperatures. Use a little more of the spices if you are going to serve it cold.

2 tablespoons butter

1 medium onion, chopped

1 apple, peeled and chopped

1 tablespoon curry powder

2 cups chicken stock

2 cups carrots, cut into
small chunks

1 cup heavy cream

1/2 teaspoon ground.hot
red pepper

Salt and pepper

❋ In a soup pot, melt the butter over medium heat. Add the onion and apple and sauté for 2 minutes. Add the curry powder and cook for 1 minute. Stir in the chicken stock and carrots. Cover and cook for 20 minutes.

❋ Using a blender or food processor, combine 1/2 cup of the cream with 1 cup of the carrot mixture and whirl away until you have a nice cream soup, about 1 minute. Transfer the mixture to a large saucepan. Repeat this process with the remaining cream and carrot mixture. Reheat the soup and correct the seasoning as needed.

Serves 6

Carrot, Ginger & Orange Soup

This soup is a beautiful orange color.

2 large carrots

1/2 yellow onion, chopped

I clementine, or half a regular orange

I quart of vegetable broth

4 pickled ginger slices, or 1/2-inch piece of fresh ginger, peeled and chopped

Salt and pepper

I teaspoon cumin

Dash of cinnamon

I½ cups of coconut milk (or other plant-based milk, or regular milk/cream)

❋ Peel and cut the carrots into 1-inch chunks and put into soup pot. Add the onion.

❋ Peel the clementine (or orange). Remove seeds. Cut into quarters and put into the pot.

❋ Add the vegetable broth. Add the ginger, salt, and pepper, and the cumin and cinnamon.

❋ Bring everything to a boil, then lower to simmer and cook until carrots are soft.

❋ Transfer half the soup to a blender with 3/4 cup of coconut milk. Whiz it up and pour into a sauce pan. Repeat with the other half of the soup, as above. Heat, correct seasonings, and serve.

Serves 6

Cream of Spinach Soup

You can adjust the amount of garlic, but the first time you cook this soup, try it with all 6 cloves.

I tablespoon olive oil

6 cloves of garlic, sliced up

I 10-ounce bag or box of frozen spinach

I½ cups vegetable broth

Salt and pepper

1/2 teaspoon nutmeg

I½ cups coconut milk (or other plant-based milk or regular milk/cream)

❋ Heat the olive oil in a frying pan with the sliced garlic on medium, and sauté until garlic is starting to brown. Add the spinach. Add half a cup of vegetable broth. Add spices, cover, and simmer until spinach is thawed and cooked, about 5 minutes.

❋ Put the spinach in a blender and add the remaining 1 cup vegetable broth and the milk.Whiz up until smooth.

❋ Return to pan to warm up and correct the seasonings. Serve HOT.

Serves 4

Cream of Wild Sorrel Soup

This is a real Adirondack soup because wild sorrel grows all over the mountains under pine trees and around dead stumps. It looks like a four-leaf clover with a heart-shaped leaf and red stem. You can substitute watercress if you don't have sorrel (you'll need two bunches of watercress or the equivalent amount of sorrel: one gallon-size resealable plastic bag full). Ok to use olive oil instead of butter, if you prefer. Instead of chicken broth, you could use vegetable broth. Instead of cream, use half-and-half, or coconut milk, or another plant-based milk.

I tablespoon butter or olive oil

I onion, chopped

One gallon-size plastic bag sorrel, washed

2 cups chicken stock

I cup heavy cream

❋ Melt the butter in a soup pot over medium heat. Add the onion and brown for 5 minutes.

❋ Add the sorrel and cover for 5 minutes or until it is wilted.

❋ Transfer it to a board and chop it up or put it through a blender with a bit of the chicken stock.

❋ Transfer the sorrel back to the soup pot and add the chicken stock, cream, and salt and pepper.

❋ Simmer for 10 minutes.

❋ Garnish with a few sorrel leaves.

Note: The stems of sorrel are red, so don't panic if the soup looks pink!

Serves 6

Cauliflower Soup

Store the whole head of cauliflower in a sealed plastic bag in the vegetable drawer of the fridge and it will last a few weeks. Do not wash it until just before use.

1 cauliflower

1 tablespoon olive oil

1 teaspoon cumin

1/4 teaspoon cinnamon

1½ cups vegetable broth

1½ cups coconut milk (or other plant-based milk, or regular milk/cream)

Salt and pepper

❊ Wash the cauliflower head. Cut off all the little flowerets and put into a caste-iron pan with the olive oil.

❊ Sauté until the pieces are turning brown in places.

❊ Add spices and stir until cauliflower pieces are coated.

❊ Transfer from frying pan to a blender.

❊ Whiz it up.

❊ Taste it, and correct seasoning.

Serves 6

Congee Chicken Soup

Calms the gut.

2 chicken breasts

1 quart of chicken stock

1½ cups rice

❊ Simmer all ingredients for two hours. Rice breaks down.

Sludge-like at end.

Serves 6

Phebe's Pioneer Stew

This recipe requires 24 hours or longer, so plan ahead!

1 large red or sweet onion

1 tablespoon butter for sautéing onion

Leftover roast beef, with bone

1 quart of vegetable broth

4 carrots, cut into one-inch pieces

1 large baking potato, cubed

1 28-ounce can of white or red beans

1 28-ounce can of stewed tomatoes

Parsley, chopped (for the stew and for serving)

Salt and pepper

❋ Go to the Pioneer Saloon (known to locals as the Pie-oh) on Main Street in Ketchum, Idaho, for dinner!

❋ Order the Pioneer-cut, bone-in (20 oz.) roast beef (medium rare), and also order a large baked potato, a steamed artichoke, and a salad. This is to fill you up so you'll have lots of leftovers!

❋ At home, get out the big stew pot. Cut the onion into tiny cubes and brown in butter.

❋ Cut off most of the meat from the bone and save about a cup of cubed beef for the stew, or use all the meat! Put the bone into the pot.

❋ Add the vegetable broth, the carrots, the beans, and the tomatoes. Add whatever spices you like, but definitely include parsley, salt, and pepper.

❋ Simmer 24 hours, covered, on VERY low heat. Add water if needed.

❋ Add cubed potatoes, and cubed meat one hour before serving, with heat turned up to low boil.

❋ Serve with chopped parsley on top. Yummy!

Serves 6

Vichyssoise

This is the classic cold potato-leek soup that is great by itself on a hot summer day and works well as a precursor to beef or veal dishes in cooler weather.

1 bunch leeks

6 tennis-ball-sized potatoes, peeled and cut into 1-inch chunks

2 cups chicken stock

1 cup half-and-half

Salt and pepper

Chopped chives or scallions for garnish

❅ Cut the leeks into 1-inch pieces and soak in cold water for 5 minutes to remove the dirt.

❅ Combine the leeks, potatoes, and chicken stock in a soup pot and simmer for 40 minutes.

❅ Using a blender or food processor, combine 1/2 cup of half-and-half with 1 cup of potato-leek mixture and blend until creamy, about 1 minute. Transfer to a large saucepan. Repeat with remaining half-and-half and potato-leek mixture.

❅ Correct the seasoning as needed. (If you serve this cold you need more seasoning than when serving it hot). Chill for 2 hours and serve with chopped chives on top.

Serves 8

Gazpacho

This is a wonderful cold, spicy summer soup of Spain. The ingredients are mixed together and chilled.

One 8-ounce can V-8 juice

6 tomatoes, chopped

1 red onion, chopped

2 cloves garlic, chopped

1 large cucumber, seeded and chopped

1 green pepper, seeded and chopped

1 teaspoon Tabasco

Salt and pepper

1 tablespoon lemon juice

❅ Combine all the ingredients in a blender or food processor and blend for 1 minute; the mixture should still be chunky.

❅ Chill for 2 hours, or all day.

❅ Serve it very cold with garnish of finely chopped tomato, green pepper, and onion.

Serves 6

Phebe's white canoe (bottom row) was named Sacagawea, and is now owned by the Morris family.

3 Bread & Pizza

Mmm . . . homemade breads and pizzas, nothing quite like it. This chapter includes a basic bread recipe that can be used for other breads, rolls, and even pizza dough. And since there were pizza pies in this chapter, I've thrown in a recipe for that classic savory pie that originated in northeastern France, quiche Lorraine, as well as the North African / Middle Eastern pie-shaped dish known as shakshuka.

BREADS

Once I made bread dough and left it in the oven (turned off) to rise, but I forgot about it so it sat there overnight. The next morning I looked in the oven and found a bowl overflowing with dough like lava out of a volcano. I dropped large spoonfuls of it onto a buttered cookie sheet, heated the oven, and baked the rolls as I usually do – they were delicious! My French friend, Beatrice told me "Oh, that is a single rising. We do that all the time in France." So once you have the yeast activated and the dough thoroughly kneaded, you can't go wrong.

Basic Bread Recipe

Bread is really easy to make and it does not take all day as many people think. Unlike pastry dough or piecrust dough, which get tough with too much handling, bread dough LOVES to be kneaded. Once you start the yeast activating by adding warm water to it, plan on about 15 minutes for the mixing and kneading. You can let it rise once or twice, or you can let it rise during the night. It's good either way, but probably a little lighter if you let it rise twice. This basic recipe can be used for pizza dough as well.

I envelope dry yeast

1½ cups warm water

3 tablespoons sugar

4 cups plus 4 tablespoons sifted flour

4 tablespoons (1/2 stick) butter, melted

❊ Put the yeast, water, sugar, and the 4 tablespoons flour in a large bowl and stir. Wait until it starts to bubble and rise a little. This will take about 15 minutes. Then stir in the rest of the flour little by little until you can make a nice ball.

❊ Put the ball of dough on a board with a thin dusting of flour on it and perhaps a cup of flour nearby to add to the board. Fold the ball in half and press down with your hand; fold it in half and press down and keep doing this kneading process for at least 10 minutes. You are activating the glutens in the flour and trapping air with each folding so the dough will rise. The ball of dough will start to have a very silky look. That's good.

❄ Put the smooth ball in the bowl, cover with a clean dish towel, and set it in a warm place with no drafts. I use the oven – an OFF oven. After about an hour or two, the dough will double in size. You can shape it into loaves, small rolls, or pizzas.

❄ Preheat the oven to 350°F.

❄ After shaping the dough as desired, place it on a buttered cookie sheet (or in a loaf pan if making a standard loaf), make a shallow cut on top with a knife (a "score") on the top of each loaf, place a towel on top, and let it rise again while the oven preheats, about 20 minutes.

❄ Drizzle the melted butter on top of each loaf to make the crusts shine. Bake for 30 to 35 minutes or until the crust is golden brown.

Makes 2 loaves, 2 pizza crusts, or 16 hard dinner rolls

Classic French Bread

❄ Use the Basic Bread Recipe on the previous page. Make the loaf long and put several diagonal scores on the top of the dough and then brush with melted butter before baking.

Makes 1 long loaf

Hearty Wheat Bread

❄ Use the Basic Bread Recipe on the previous page, substituting a mixture of 1/2 sifted white flour and 1/2 sifted whole wheat flour. Make the loaves rounder and put 3 scores across the top. Melted butter on top is optional.

Makes 2 loaves

Dinner Rolls

❄ Use the Basic Bread Recipe on the previous page. Make dough balls about 2 inches in diameter and place them on greased cookie sheets. Score the tops with one cut and baste with butter. Serve warm.

Makes 16 rolls

Skillet Corn Bread

Here's another Kenneth recipe – true camp cooking.

3 tablespoons butter

1 cup cornmeal

1 cup flour

1/4 cup sugar

1 tablespoon baking powder

1/2 teaspoon salt

1 egg

1 cup milk

1 tablespoon molasses
or maple syrup

1 cup corn kernels

❊ Preheat the oven to 350°F.

❊ Melt the butter in a cast-iron skillet. You can let butter melt in the oven or on top of stove. You want the oven and the skillet HOT when you pour the batter in.

❊ Mix all the remaining ingredients together in a bowl and let it sit for 10 minutes.

❊ Pour the batter into the hot skillet. Bake for 25 minutes or until golden brown.

Serves 6

Banana Bread

This is a great way to use overripe bananas. For dessert, fry slices of this bread in butter and top with ice cream.

2 bananas, very ripe

2 eggs

1/4 cup molasses

1/4 cup brown sugar

2 cups flour

1 teaspoon baking soda

1 teaspoon cinnamon

Dash of nutmeg

1/4 cup chopped nuts

1/4 cup orange juice

1/4 cup melted butter

❊ Preheat the oven to 350°F.

❊ In a bowl, mash the bananas with a fork. I use a fork from start to finish. Add the eggs and mix. Add the molasses and brown sugar. Mix. Add the flour, baking soda, spices, nuts, and finally the melted butter and orange juice, mix well.

❊ Pour the batter into a buttered loaf pan (4 x 9 inch) or a muffin tin and let it sit for 15 to 20 minutes to let it rise slightly.

❊ Bake for 60 minutes or until a knife goes in and out clean (for muffins bake 40 minutes). Let bread cool 15 minutes before removing from pan.

Makes 1 loaf or 10 to 12 muffins

When I visited Italy in 1960, no Italian that I met had ever heard of a pizza. So my theory is that an Italian immigrant was making a tomato quiche and the piecrust came out thinner and crispier than expected. He served it as he would a slice of quiche, saying, "Have a piece of pie," only it came out, "Have a piz' a pie." The pizza pie was born! Here are recipes for three pizzas, but with a little imagination and some different toppings, the possibilities are endless.

Basic Pizza

This sauce for the pizza is also good on pasta.

**1 Basic Bread Recipe
(page 124)**

**1 recipe Tomato (Pomodoro)
Sauce (page 134)**

POSSIBLE TOPPINGS:

**8 ounces mozzarella cheese,
shredded**

**8 ounces grated
Parmesan cheese, grated**

❉ **Basic Directions:** The basic bread recipe on page 124 makes two 12-inch pizza crusts. After the kneading and one rising, pre-heat the oven to 475°F. (The oven needs to be very hot before you cook the pizza, so don't skip this step.)

❉ Make two dough balls. Flatten and stretch each ball onto an oiled pizza pan, or you can toss it on your floured hands if you have the guts. You want the dough to be thin, with a small crust along the edge.

❉ Spread the sauce on the dough, and then distribute your toppings over it.

❉ Bake in the middle shelf for 15 minutes (unless directed otherwise in the recipes).

Makes two 12-inch pizzas

Pesto & Goat Cheese Pizza

A red, white, and green pizza – the colors of the Italian flag.

**1 Basic Bread Recipe
(page 124)**

1 cup pesto (page 136)

2 beefsteak tomatoes, sliced thin

8 ounces soft goat cheese

4 sun-dried tomatoes, diced

**2 cups shredded mozzarella
cheese**

❄ Prepare the dough according to the basic directions on the previous page.

❄ Preheat the oven to 425°F.

❄ Spread the pesto on the dough. Place a thin layer of sliced tomatoes on the pesto. Dot with blobs of goat cheese. Sprinkle the sun-dried tomatoes around and then sprinkle the mozzarella on top.

❄ Bake for 15 minutes, or until the cheese is melted and the crust is brown.

Makes two 12-inch pizzas

Spinach & Feta Pizza

My son and daughter-in-law have a pizza parlor, but even Mom can't get the recipes. This recipe is adapted from watching.

**1 Basic Bread Recipe
(page 124)**

6 tablespoons virgin olive oil

2 boxes frozen, chopped spinach

4 cloves garlic, minced

8 ounces feta cheese

8 ounces Parmesan cheese, grated

❄ Prepare the dough according to the basic directions on the previous page.

❄ Preheat the oven to 425°F.

❄ Spread the oil on the dough. Microwave the spinach for 2 minutes and, when it has cooled, squeeze out all liquid.

❄ Spread the garlic and spinach over the oil. Sprinkle the feta on top, then the Parmesan.

❄ Bake for 15 minutes.

Makes two 12-inch pizzas

Classic Quiche

This is a recipe for classic quiche lorraine. It's easy to come up with variations to use your leftovers, such as cooked broccoli, asparagus, ham, or shrimp. Since this is camp, I use the frozen piecrusts.

2 eggs

3 egg yolks

2¼ cups heavy cream

1 teaspoon Dijon mustard

Dash of cayenne pepper

1 teaspoon dry mustard

1/4 cup grated Parmesan cheese

1/2 cup grated Swiss cheese
(half Gruyère & half Emmenthaler
works best)

1/4 teaspoon nutmeg

Salt and pepper

One 10-inch frozen piecrust,
thawed

❋ Preheat the oven to 350°F.

❋ Mix all the ingredients in a bowl and pour into a 10-inch pie dish lined with the piecrust. (For variations, spread cooked vegetables with 1 chopped onion on the piecrust and then pour the egg and cheese mixture over them.)

❋ Bake for about 45 minutes. The quiche is done when the top is brown and the pie barely jiggles when you move it. It will firm up as it cools.

❋ Let it sit for 10 minutes before serving.

Note: If the ingredients are cold when you make the filling, the quiche may take longer to cook.

Serves 6

Shakshuka with Eggs & Feta

On Christmas morning, Peter Boyle cooked this for us, but he added sliced sausages.

3 tablespoons olive oil

I large yellow onion, chopped

3 cloves of garlic sliced

I teaspoon cumin

I teaspoon paprika

1/8 teaspoon cayenne pepper

28-ounce can stewed tomatoes

Salt and pepper

5 ounces feta cheese crumbles

6 eggs

Chopped cilantro,
for serving

❄ Turn on oven at 375 degrees.

❄ Get out your biggest cast-iron frying pan. Put in the olive oil and the chopped onion and sauté on medium-high until the onion is soft. Add garlic and cumin and paprika and cayenne, and stir, cook for 2 minutes.

❄ Add the tomatoes, and salt and pepper. Simmer for 10 minutes, stirring now and again.

❄ Stir in the feta cheese. Crack open and drop the eggs around the edge. Put into preheated oven for 10 minutes.

❄ Serve with chopped cilantro sprinkled on top.

Serves 6

Leftovers: The tomato sauce with melted feta makes a delicious tomato soup with vegetable broth and coconut milk. Whiz it up in blender and serve.

*Thorne owls everywhere! In the mid 1800s, the Thorne coat of arms had become so complicated
(and difficult to reproduce) that they threw out everything and decided from then on the family crest would be a winking owl.
This little bird with big eyes is a saw-whet owl.*

4 Pasta, Potatoes, Rice

Since you can do so many things with pasta, it is a wonderful staple to have on hand. And a box of dried pasta can sit on a shelf almost forever. Italians often eat pasta as a separate course before the meat or fish course. At camp, we usually serve it as a main dish. In any event, here are some good recipes to get you started.

Pasta

Potatoes

Rice

Tomato (Pomodoro) Sauce

One fall, I rented a house in Tuscany, Italy. At the bottom of the hill was a little grocery store. I bought fresh pasta made by the owner, six ripe tomatoes, a bunch of fresh basil, a small tube of tomato paste, a chunk of local Parmesan, and a bottle of local olive oil. I made this pomodoro sauce in 20 minutes and it was the best I had ever tasted. Of course the tomatoes were ripe, the olive oil extremely tasty, and the local Parmesan and basil beyond comparison. As with all cooking, fresh and ripe ingredients are very important. Pick out the ripest tomatoes, spend the extra money for real Italian Parmesan from Parma, use a good grade of virgin Italian oil, use fresh, crisp basil, and fresh pasta if it is available. The results will be worth it!

Virgin olive oil

I head of garlic, cloves peeled and minced

One 12-ounce can Italian tomatoes or 6 ripe tomatoes diced

A bunch of fresh basil or oregano, or I tablespoon dried

Pinch of cinnamon

Salt and pepper

I small can tomato paste

❄ In a cast-iron skillet, sauté the garlic in a little olive oil over medium heat. Add the tomatoes, basil, cinnamon, and salt and pepper to taste. Simmer for 1 hour if you use canned tomatoes. Simmer for 20 minutes if you use fresh tomatoes.

❄ Add tomato paste to thicken the sauce to the desired consistency: spreadable for pizza, pourable for pasta. You will probably need only 3 to 4 tablespoons (it will depend on the juice in the tomatoes you use).

Serves 4, enough for 1 pound pasta or 2 pizzas

Bolognese Sauce

I learned this recipe from my Italian teacher; she explained that every household has its own version of this sauce. Basically, it is ground meat, tomatoes, garlic, and herbs cooked for hours. I find that if you add ground pork, parsley, and cinnamon, the base is very rich. For the pork, you can use the inside of sweet Italian sausage.

2 tablespoons olive oil

1 large onion, chopped

1/2 head garlic, minced

1 pound ground beef (the better the meat, the better the sauce)

1/2 pound ground pork

6 to 8 large tomatoes, chopped or 2 cans Italian tomatoes, or 3 cups chopped tomatoes, fresh and canned mixed

1 bunch parsley, chopped

2 tablespoons dried basil or 6 sprigs fresh basil

Pinch of cinnamon

Salt and pepper

1 small can tomato paste

❉ In a cast-iron skillet, heat the olive oil over medium heat and sauté the onions, garlic, and meat until the meat is brown, about 10 minutes.

❉ Transfer the mixture to a soup pot and add the tomatoes, parsley, basil, cinnamon, and salt and pepper to taste. Simmer for at least 30 minutes. Thicken with the tomato paste as needed.

Serves 8; enough for 2 boxes pasta

Pesto

This sauce is basil, pine nuts, garlic, and olive oil whizzed in the blender. It's good on pasta or pizza, and as an ingredient any time a recipe calls for basil and oil. You can store it in the refrigerator in a glass jar for three weeks.

2 bunches basil (or quart-size resealable plastic bag full)

8 cloves garlic

1/2 cup pine nuts

1 cup virgin olive oil

❄ Discard the basil stems. Whiz all the ingredients together in the blender or food processor for 2 minutes.

❄ This is enough for a box of pasta. Toss it on hot, cooked pasta. Add salt and pepper and serve with Parmesan.

Serves 4

Spaghetti with Meatballs

Spaghetti with meatballs is a pomodoro sauce with meatballs that are made like a meat loaf. So start by making the meatballs first; you can use the meat loaf recipe or you can use leftover meat loaf cut into small chunks. If you use leftover meat loaf the "balls" will be little cubes instead. It tastes just as good!

I recipe Tomato (Pomodoro)
Sauce (page 134)

I recipe Meat Loaf (page 77)

4 tablespoons olive oil

I package dried spaghetti

Freshly grated Parmesan cheese

❄ Prepare the tomato sauce as directed in the recipe.

❄ Prepare the meat loaf as directed in the recipe, but instead of forming a loaf, form the mixture into balls the size of marbles or ping-pong balls. Put them on a plate and refrigerate for 15 minutes (this will keep them from falling apart as you fry them).

❄ Heat the olive oil in a cast-iron skillet. Add the meatballs and fry until brown on all sides. Add the meatballs to the sauce to cook for 15 minutes more.

❄ Cook the spaghetti according to the directions on the package. You can cook it a little less than recommended — pasta is best served al dente (firm).

❄ Serve the sauce and meatballs over the cooked pasta. Don't forget to put fresh grated Parmesan on top of each serving.

Serves 4–6

Spaghetti Carbonara

My friend, Cuca, Baroness Cararra, stayed with me in New York and showed me how to do this classic Italian workman's pasta. Her husband's family owns the Cararra marble quarry where all of the great Italian sculptors got their marble. Michelangelo's David is made of Cararra marble. I imagine the quarry workers going home to sip wine and eat this pasta.

I pound bacon

I pound spaghetti

8 tablespoons (I stick) butter, very soft

2 tablespoons milk

2 eggs

I tablespoon heavy cream

1/2 cup grated Parmesan cheese

Chopped parsley, for garnish, about 2 tablespoons

Salt and pepper

❋ Cook the bacon in a cast-iron skillet until crisp. Drain on paper towels and crumble into pieces.

❋ Cook the spaghetti according to the directions on the package. While it is cooking, whisk together the butter, milk, eggs, and cream in a warm bowl.

❋ Drain the spaghetti, transfer it to the bowl with the egg mixture, and toss to combine. The hot pasta will cook the egg onto the pasta. Stir in the bacon and Parmesan. Season with salt and pepper to taste. Top with the parsley before serving.

Serves 4

Pasta with Garlic Oil & Vegetables

Since you always have garlic, oil, pasta, and Parmesan in the kitchen, any fresh vegetable you find will combine with these staples to make a total meal. You can use ziti, bowties, spaghetti – any pasta you want.

1 pound pasta

1 cup good olive oil

12 cloves garlic, thinly sliced

1 yellow squash, cut into
bite-size pieces

1 zucchini, cut into bite-size pieces

1 green or red bell pepper, cut
into bite-size pieces

1 large sweet onion, sliced

12 cherry tomatoes

1 tablespoon dried basil
or oregano or leaves
from 2 sprigs fresh

Salt and pepper

1/2 cup grated Parmesan cheese

❋ Cook the pasta according to the directions on the package.

❋ While the pasta is cooking, heat the oil with the garlic in a cast-iron skillet until it is hot and begins to sizzle.

❋ Add the vegetables, basil, and salt and pepper to taste and sauté for 3 minutes.

❋ Cover the pan, lower the heat, and cook for 7 minutes.

❋ Add the cooked pasta and toss to combine.

❋ Transfer the pasta from the skillet to a warm bowl. Serve with the Parmesan cheese on top.

Serves 4–6

The Uplands cocktail porch

Vegetable Lasagna

This recipe is dedicated to Sallie Ann and Bob Hart, who sent me the following review: "This is our Phebe! Yesterday you were up to making the most delicious lasagna we have ever tasted. It melted in our mouths. So creamy, and beautifully seasoned. Thank you for sharing your culinary genius!"

FOR THE SAUCE

1 tablespoon olive oil

1 head of garlic peeled, minced

28-ounce can stewed tomatoes

2 tablespoons dried basil

Pinch of cinnamon

Salt and pepper to taste

FOR THE LASAGNA

2 tablespoons butter or olive oil

1 sweet large onion, diced

1 green or red bell pepper, diced

1 stalk of celery, diced

1 10-ounce box or bag frozen chopped spinach, (thawed)

1 10-ounce bag frozen peas

2 tablespoons dried basil leaves

16 ounces of Parmesan cheese, grated

8 ounces ricotta cheese

8 ounces sour cream

4 ounces cream cheese, softened

1 pound lasagna noodles. Use regular or no-boil noodles.

8 ounces mozzarella cheese, sliced

Salt and pepper

❄ **For the sauce:** In a cast-iron skillet, sauté the garlic in the olive oil over medium heat until softened.

❄ Add the tomatoes and herbs and simmer on medium heat for 20 to 30 minutes, uncovered, stirring often.

❄ Add 3 to 4 tablespoons tomato paste to thicken so that it is pourable but not watery.

❄ Simmer for another 5 minutes.

❄ **For the lasagna:** Turn on the oven to 350 degrees.

❄ In a bowl, mix the 4 cheeses.

❄ In a cast-iron skillet, sauté the onion over medium heat until just turning soft and translucent.

❄ Add the celery and cook 2 minutes.

❄ Add red pepper, stir, then spinach, stir.

❄ Add peas, stir, and then turn off the heat. All the veggies will cook a lot more in the oven.

❄ Oil or butter the bottom of an 9 X 13-inch lasagna pan.

❄ Cover the bottom with noodles, and then layer: 1/2 the vegetable mixture, 1/2 the tomato sauce, and 1/2 the cheese mixture.

❄ Repeat: noodles, veggies, sauce, cheese.

❄ Top with overlapping mozzarella slices.

❄ Bake for 45 minutes at 350 degrees or until lasagna bubbles up from bottom and cheese on the top is golden. If using regular noodles, cover with aluminum foil for the first 30 minutes.

❋ Let the lasagna sit outside the oven for 5 minutes before you cut into it.

Serves 6 as a main course or 8–10 as a side dish

Note: *This is even better if you make it up a day ahead and refrigerate it. The layers stick together better and the flavors meld nicely. If you bake it straight from the refrigerator, add 15 to 20 minutes to the cooking time.*

Variation: For **meat lasagna**, use Bolognese Sauce instead of the tomatoes and vegetables, but prepare the garlic as indicated above, and add the cinnamon.

Pasta Primavera

This ingredient list looks a lot like the one in the previous recipe. The difference is that pasta primavera has a cream sauce that gives it a very different flavor. Don't be afraid to experiment with different vegetables that you may have in your refrigerator. This is a great way to use leftover vegetables.

1 pound pasta

2 tablespoons butter

1 clove garlic, minced

1 zucchini, cut into
bite-size pieces

1 yellow squash, cut into
bite-size pieces

1 green bell pepper, cut into
bite-size pieces

12 cherry tomatoes, cut in half

1 sweet onion (Vidalia, Maui,
or red), sliced

1 tablespoon dried basil
or oregano (or both)
or leaves from 2 sprigs fresh

Salt and pepper

2 cups heavy cream

1/2 cup grated Parmesan cheese

❋ Cook the pasta according to the directions on the package.

❋ While the pasta is cooking, melt the butter in the cast-iron skillet, and sauté the garlic for 1 to 2 minutes.

❋ Add all the vegetables and sauté for 5 minutes.

❋ Stir in the basil, salt and pepper to taste, and cream.

❋ Bring the mixture to a boil, then let boil for 1 minute.

❋ Remove from the heat.

❋ Add the cooked pasta, toss.

❋ Serve from the skillet, or a warm bowl, with the Parmesan cheese on top.

Serves 4–6

Linguine with Clam Sauce

This is a favorite, an easy main-course dish. This recipe and a simple green salad make for a wonderful and easy casual meal. To remove the skins from the garlic cloves, place them on a hard surface and crush them with the side of a chef's knife. The skins will come off easily and the cloves will be ready to chop.

Two 10-ounce cans whole baby clams (or 30 fresh clams)

One 10-ounce can or two 4-ounce cans chopped clams

4 tablespoons butter

2 tablespoons olive oil

6 cloves garlic, chopped

I package dried (or fresh) linguine

I bunch parsley leaves, minced

I teaspoon dried basil (or I tablespoon chopped basil leaves)

1/2 teaspoon dried oregano

1/2 teaspoon coarsely ground pepper

1/4 cup heavy cream (optional)

Grated Parmesan cheese

❄ Strain the juices from the canned clams and set it aside.

❄ Cook the linguine according to the directions on the package.

❄ In a one-quart saucepan, heat the butter and olive oil over medium heat. Add the garlic and sauté for 3 to 4 minutes.

❄ Add the chopped clams, then the whole clams. Add a little of the clam juice to thin it and for flavor.

❄ Add the parsley, oregano, pepper, basil, and a bit more clam juice to the skillet.

❄ Add the cream and simmer for 3 to 5 minutes.

❄ Put the cooked pasta in a large bowl, pour the sauce over it, and toss together with two large spoons.

❄ Serve with Parmesan on top.

Serves 4

Macaroni & Cheese

This is the kids' all-time favorite dinner when cooked over an open fire. If you are cooking this outside, you'll need a pot to boil the macaroni. The "baking" portion is over hot coals in the covered skillet.

One 8-ounce box macaroni

2 tablespoons butter

2 medium sweet onions, chopped

2 teaspoons chili powder

2 tablespoons flour

2 cups half-and-half

2 teaspoons salt

2 teaspoons pepper

Pinch of nutmeg

2 cups grated hard cheeses,
such as cheddar and Parmesan

Breadcrumbs and butter
for topping

❄ Preheat the oven to 350°F.

❄ Cook the macaroni in boiling water for 8 minutes. Drain and place in a casserole dish.

❄ In a skillet, melt the butter and sauté the onion until it is clear. Add the chili powder and flour and sauté until it balls up.

❄ Add the half-and-half, nutmeg, and salt and pepper to taste.

❄ Pour the sauce over the macaroni and mix in the cheeses.

❄ Top with a thin layer of breadcrumbs and dots of butter.

❄ Bake for 20 minutes or until the sauce is bubbling.

Serves 4

Pasta with Brussels Sprouts & Bacon

This recipe is a 21st-century version of comfort food!

8 slices of bacon,
cooked until crisp

8 ounces of short, twisty pasta

2 shallots, diced

12 Brussels sprouts, ends cut off
and outer leaves removed, then
cut in half

1 tablespoon olive oil

1/4 cup red wine vinegar

1 tablespoon Dijon mustard

1 14½-ounce can
of stewed tomatoes

1½ teaspoon red pepper flakes

Shaved Parmesan cheese, to serve

❄ In your cast iron fry pan, fry the bacon until it is golden and crispy.

❄ When bacon is crispy, remove it from the pan, leaving in 2 tablespoons of grease.

❄ Cook the pasta in a pot of boiling water (or cook it later, if you are cooking the Brussels sprouts ahead of time).

❄ In the fry pan, cook the shallots and Brussels sprouts (start with cut side down) until sprouts start to crisp up and brown.

❄ Add the vinegar and mustard and stir it up.

❄ Add the tomatoes and red pepper flakes and stir, scraping the bottom of the pan. If the pan gets too dry, add some more olive oil or some pasta water.

❄ To serve, toss vegetables with pasta.

❄ Crumble the bacon over the top.

❄ Arrange shaved Parmesan cheese on top, or serve it in a separate bowl.

Serves 4

Potatoes Dauphinoise

My French friend, Beatrice, taught me this recipe. It is like scalloped potatoes but without the cheese. It is a perfect dish to go with a roast or grilled meat. If you have some left over, you can reheat it and serve it with eggs and bacon the next morning.

5 to 6 tablespoons butter

1 clove garlic

2 potatoes the size of tennis balls

1 cup heavy cream mixed with 1/2 cup sour cream

Salt and pepper

❋ Preheat the oven to 350°F.

❋ Rub the bottom of a large class lasagna pan with 1 tablespoon of the butter. Then rub the peeled clove of garlic around in the butter to flavor it (you can also mince the garlic and sprinkle it around).

❋ Slice the potatoes VERY thin. Use a mandoline if you have it, but be careful.

❋ Layer the potatoes in the pan with dots of butter and salt and pepper between the layers.

❋ Pour the cream mixture around the sides. You may have to add more cream if the potatoes soak it up fast while cooking.

❋ Bake for 45 minutes to 1 hour, until the potatoes are soft when poked with a sharp knife. It should be a little brown on top and bubble around the sides when done.

Serves 6

Potato-Onion Pie

This is a little like a quiche and a little like potatoes Anna in a pie shell. It is great with grilled meat or for lunch with cold leftover meats or with a big Caesar salad.

1 piecrust (use a frozen one; thaw first)

2 potatoes, sliced very thin (use the mandoline if you have one)

2 medium sweet onions (Maui, Vidalia or red), thinly sliced

1/4 teaspoon nutmeg

Salt and pepper

1 egg beaten with 1/2 cup cream

1 tablespoon butter

❄ Preheat the oven to 350°F.

❄ Place the piecrust in a pie plate. Arrange the potatoes and onions in the pie crust. Season with the nutmeg, salt, and pepper. Pour the egg-cream mixture on top. Dot with the butter.

❄ Bake for 45 minutes or until the center is firm.

Serves 6

Phebe on the trail

Potatoes Anna

This may be the very first "elegant" potato dish I learned as a young bride. This dish consists of layers of very thin slices of potato with butter in between cooked on top of the stove slowly until the potatoes stick together. When you flip it over onto a plate and sprinkle chopped parsley on top, you have a beautiful pie to serve with any meat.

4 tablespoons butter

4 Idaho or Yukon gold potatoes, sliced very thin (use a mandoline if you have one)

Salt and pepper

2 tablespoons chopped parsley, for garnish

❊ In an omelet pan with sloping sides, melt 1 tablespoon of the butter over low heat.

❊ Add a layer of potatoes by starting in the center and fanning and overlapping the slices a little like a pinwheel. This will be the top when it's cooked and the potatoes have been turned upside down onto a big plate.

❊ Dot the potatoes with bits of butter and season with salt and pepper.

❊ Place another layer of potatoes on top and repeat the butter and salt and pepper.

❊ Continue until you have about 3 or 4 layers. Use a spatula and shake the pan to be sure the bottom is not sticking while you layer the potatoes.

❊ Cover and continue to cook over very low heat for 20 to 30 minutes. It's done when a knife goes in easily.

❊ Take the pan off the heat and carefully lift around the bottom with the spatula to be sure nothing is stuck.

❊ Place a large plate on top and flip the pan so the potato "pie" falls onto the plate.

❊ Sprinkle chopped parsley on top.

❊ To serve, cut into wedges.

Serves 6

Potato Pancakes

These are good for breakfast or lunch or as a side dish with leftover cold meat. What better way is there to use up leftover mashed potatoes? Serve with a bowl of sweet onions, a bowl of sour cream, and a bowl of applesauce.

FOR THE PANCAKES

I cup mashed potatoes

I cup Bisquick

I cup milk

I egg

1/2 onion, chopped

4 tablespoons butter

FOR THE ONIONS

I tablespoon butter

I onion, thinly sliced

I teaspoon balsamic vinegar

I tablespoon sugar

FOR THE APPLESAUCE

2 apples, cut into small pieces
(I don't peel mine)

1/2 cup sugar

I teaspoon cinnamon

1/4 teaspoon nutmeg

I tablespoon lemon or lime juice
(even orange juice will do)

❊ **To make the pancakes:** Mix the potatoes, Bisquick, milk, egg, and onion together in a bowl. Let the batter sit for at least 15 minutes so it rises a little. This will help make fluffy pancakes. While you're waiting, prepare the onions and applesauce.

❊ **To prepare the onions:** Melt the butter over medium heat in a cast-iron skillet. Add the onion and until translucent.

❊ Add the sugar and cook until it melts.

❊ Add the vinegar and turn off the heat.

❊ Transfer to a small bowl for serving.

❊ **To make the applesauce:** Mix all the applesauce ingredients in a saucepan and cook while you make the pancakes. Cook over low to medium heat, uncovered, for 30 minutes stirring 3 or 4 times. It will thicken as it cools and will be chunky. If you like a smooth applesauce, cook it a little longer.

❊ Cook the pancakes 4 or 5 at a time in butter on a hot griddle. Transfer to a platter and keep warm in the oven while you cook the rest of the pancakes.

Serves 6–8

Quick Sauté of Potatoes, Apples, & Onions

I first cooked this on top of a mountain over an open fire to accompany a steak dinner. Use a cast-iron skillet for this dish.

4 tablespoons butter

2 potatoes (Idaho or Yukon gold are best), peeled and cut into 1/4-inch-thick slices

2 medium onions, sliced

2 apples, sliced

❋ Melt the butter in a cast-iron skillet over medium heat. Add the potatoes and cook over until almost done, about 7 minutes. Flip them often with a spatula or spoon. Add the onions and cook for 5 minutes. Add the apples and cook 5 minutes more, stirring often. Season with salt and pepper to taste.

Serves 4

Soubise

This is a rich combination of rice, onion, cream, and cheese. The French make this with leftover rice. It is delicious with steak, chicken, or grilled kebobs.

4 tablespoons butter

3 sweet onions, cut in half and sliced very thin

1 cup cooked (or leftover) rice

1 cup heavy cream

1/2 cup grated Parmesan cheese

Salt and Pepper

❋ In a cast-iron skillet, melt the butter over medium heat. Add the onions and sauté until they are translucent.

❋ Add the rice and cream and stir well. Cook for 4 to 5 minutes. Add the Parmesan cheese stirring until the cheese has melted. Season with salt and pepper to taste.

Serves 6

5 Meat & Fish

Always remember the motto "KISS," for Keep It Simple Stupid. When serving a more complicated main dish such as lasagna, cassoulet, or duck à l'orange, plan a simple vegetable dish, such as a salad and baked potatoes or boiled rice. If your main course is grilled or roasted meat, go ahead and do the veggie stacks or a salad mold. Included here are the recipes for leftovers from the six dinners found in Chapter 1.

Chicken Divan

My mother was a terrible cook. While growing up, we had Molly, a great Irish cook, but she was off on Thursdays. Mom would take a casserole dish and throw all the week's leftovers into it, top it with a can of cream of mushroom soup, and bake it for dinner – AWFUL. We begged to go out for dinner on Thursdays. In 1972, Mom married Chuck and thought it was silly to have a cook for just two people, so she learned a few basic recipes. This is a good one.

2 boneless chicken breasts, cut in half (4 pieces)

Flour for dredging

2 tablespoons butter

1 medium onion, chopped

1/2 cup white wine or champagne

1/2 cup water

1 bunch broccoli, cut into bite-size pieces

1 pint heavy cream

1 teaspoon thyme

Salt and pepper

1/4 cup slivered almonds

1/4 cup breadcrumbs

❋ Preheat the oven to 350°F.

❋ Wash the chicken and pat it dry. Dredge the pieces in flour and shake off the excess.

❋ Melt the butter in a cast-iron skillet over medium heat. Brown the chicken for 7 minutes on each side. Remove the chicken from the skillet.

❋ Add the onion and sauté until it is translucent.

❋ Stir in the wine and let it bubble for 1 minute. Add the water, cover the pan, lower the heat, and simmer for 20 minutes.

❋ In a small saucepan, boil the broccoli for 5 minutes (or microwave it for 3 minutes) and drain. Transfer the broccoli to a flat, ovenproof dish. Lay the chicken on top.

❋ Bring the sauce to a boil and cook until reduced to 1 cup. Stir in the cream, thyme, and salt and pepper to taste. Pour over the chicken. Top with the almonds and breadcrumbs.

❋ Bake for 30 minutes or until the casserole is bubbly and the topping has browned.

Serves 4

Classic Sautéed Chicken Breasts

This sauté recipe is good for chicken or veal. It's quick and easy and absolutely delicious. A sauté pan has three-inch straight sides; it's heavy and has a tight lid. Your cast-iron skillet will do fine if you have a cover that fits.

2 boneless chicken breasts,
cut in half (4 pieces)

4 tablespoons butter, softened

Flour for dredging

1 cup white wine

1 cup water

1 bunch scallions

1 teaspoon thyme

Salt and pepper

❊ Wash the chicken and pat it dry. Dredge it in the flour and shake off the excess.

❊ Melt 2 tablespoons of the butter in a sauté pan over medium heat. Add the chicken, and brown both sides quickly, about 7 minutes per side. Remove the chicken from the pan.

❊ Chop the white part of the scallions, and place them in the sauté pan (save the green parts for the garnish). Cook for 3 minutes.

❊ Stir in the wine and let it boil for 2 minutes. Add the water, thyme, and salt and pepper to taste.

❊ Put the chicken back in the pan. Lower the heat, cover the pan with a tight lid, and simmer for 20 minutes.

❊ Transfer the chicken to a warm platter. Boil the pan juices down until they are reduced to 1 cup. Turn off the heat.

❊ Add the remaining 2 tablespoons butter and tip the pan back and forth until the butter melts into the sauce and thickens it. Don't whisk or stir vigorously; maybe stir with a fork gently.

❊ To serve, pour the sauce over the chicken and garnish with chopped scallion tops.

Serves 4

Grilled & Marinated Chicken

This marinade works equally well on a 1½-pound flank or skirt steak. Just turn down the heat to medium instead of low for the second part of the cooking.

2 boneless chicken breasts,
cut in half (4 pieces)

FOR THE MARINADE

1 cup olive oil

1/3 cup red wine (or any) vinegar

1 tablespoon dried basil

1 tablespoon dried rosemary

2 tablespoons coarsely ground
pepper

1 tablespoon salt

6 cloves garlic, diced

1 small sweet onion, diced

1 tablespoon Liquid Smoke
or lime juice (optional)

❋ Wash the chicken and pat it dry with a paper towel.

❋ Put the chicken breasts and all of the marinade ingredients in a gallon-size resealable plastic bag. Seal the bag and slosh it around to mix well. Let the air out of the bag, reseal, and let stand for 3 hours.

❋ You may marinate the chicken a day or two ahead but keep it in the refrigerator until three hours before cooking.

❋ Preheat the grill to high.

❋ Grill the chicken for 1½ minutes per side.

❋ Turn heat to low and cook for an additional 5 to 7 minutes per side.

❋ Serve sliced or whole.

Serves 4

Fried Chicken with Cream Gravy

Evelyn came to work for me as my daughter Helena's nanny in November 1981. I found out by accident that she had previously worked as a cook at a luncheonette in Birmingham, Alabama. I was taking exams at law school and she asked if she could help by cooking dinner. Fried chicken with cream gravy and rice were waiting for the family when we arrived home from work, exams, and school. That was the first of many southern dishes Evelyn cooked for us.

FOR THE CHICKEN

I fryer, cut into 8 pieces

I cup flour in a brown paper bag

2 cups vegetable oil

FOR THE GRAVY

2 tablespoons butter

2 tablespoons flour

2 cups milk

Salt and pepper

❅ Wash the chicken and pat it dry. Put 2 or 3 pieces of chicken into the paper bag with flour and shake until the pieces are coated. Repeat with the remaining pieces.

❅ Heat the oil in a heavy, high-sided pan. The oil should be so hot that a piece of chicken or ball of flour and water sizzles into a brown ball in 10 seconds. Put 3 pieces at a time into the hot oil and fry for 10 minutes until brown, the oil should crackle.

❅ Transfer the cooked chicken to drain on paper towels or another brown paper bag in a warm oven. Repeat the process with the rest of the chicken.

❅ When all the pieces are cooked, pour off the oil into a clean coffee can (you can use it again in a few days). Save the little brown pieces of fried skin and flour on the bottom – the crunchies – which you will add to the cream gravy.

❅ To make the gravy, melt the butter in a cast-iron skillet. Add the flour and cook until it forms a ball. Whisk in the milk and let it boil until it thickens. Add salt, lots of black pepper, and the crunchies.

❅ Whisk the gravy until smooth. Serve in a warm pitcher.

Serves 6

Cold Hacked Chicken

This is an interesting and different way to use leftover chicken.

1 cooked chicken (roasted or rotisserie), cooled

1 tablespoon vegetable oil

1 tablespoon dried red pepper flakes

1-inch piece of ginger root, peeled and finely chopped

3 cloves garlic, chopped

1 zucchini, sliced

4 tablespoons soy sauce

1 teaspoon sesame oil

2 scallions, chopped

❄ Cut all the chicken off the bones, then shred it, cut it, or pull it apart. If the pieces look like shreds or funny blobs, don't worry, it's "hacked chicken." Place the chicken in a pretty serving dish.

❄ In a cast-iron skillet, heat the oil over medium heat with the red pepper flakes until they turn very dark. Remove the pepper flakes with a slotted spoon and discard them. Add the ginger, garlic, and zucchini. Cover and cook for 3 minutes. Add the soy sauce and sesame oil.

❄ Pour the sauce over the chicken.

Serves 6–8

Arbor in The Uplands garden

Chicken Pot Pie

You can use any ovenproof dish or glass pie pan or even a brownie pan. If you brush the top of the crust with butter or a beaten egg white before baking, it will brown with a shine. If I have any piecrust left over, I use a cute cookie cutter and put a star or rooster or dog in the center. (I use frozen crusts. This is camp cooking after all. Thaw the crust before using.)

I tablespoon butter

I large onion, chopped

I potato, peeled and diced

I stalk celery, chopped

2 carrots sliced, or 10 baby carrots cut in half

I tablespoon flour

I cup half-and-half

1/2 cup leftover gravy or chicken stock

2 cups leftover chicken, cut into bite-size pieces

1/2 package frozen peas

I piecrust

❄ Preheat the oven to 350°F.

❄ In a cast-iron skillet, melt the butter over medium heat. Add the onion and cook until brown. Add the potato and cook for 5 minutes. Add more butter if the pan looks dry. Add the celery and carrots and sauté for 5 minutes.

❄ Add the flour and whisk as it balls up into a roux. Add the milk and the gravy. Keep whisking.

❄ Stir in the chicken and the peas and cook for 2 minutes to heat up the chicken and cook the peas.

❄ Pour the mixture into an ovenproof dish. Top with the piecrust. Make 3 little slashes in the crust so hot air can escape during cooking.

❄ Bake for 40 minutes or until the crust is light brown and the pie is bubbling.

❄ Serve with Cranberry Compote (page 81).

Serves 4

Chicken Salad

You can serve this on lettuce for lunch or as a sandwich. If you can't find grapes, chop up an apple.

2 cups cubed cooked chicken

I bunch scallions chopped (or a
red onion, chopped)

1/2 cup green or red seedless
grapes, cut in half

1/4 cup walnuts or pecans

I cup mayonnaise mixed with
2 tablespoons lemon juice

I tablespoon fresh thyme,
oregano, or basil

Salt and pepper

1/4 teaspoon curry powder

❈ Mix all the ingredients together in a bowl and refrigerate. Serve on lettuce with bread or rolls.

Serves 4

Chicken Hash

I've been to some fancy clubs in New York City where I see this comfort food on the menu for the stressed bankers, lawyers, and financiers!

2 tablespoons butter

I potato, cut into 1/2-inch cubes

I medium onion, chopped

I green or red bell pepper,
chopped

I cup cut-up cooked chicken

1/2 cup leftover gravy (use cream
with 2 tablespoons soy sauce if
you don't have gravy)

Salt and pepper

❈ In a cast-iron skillet, melt the butter over medium heat. Add the potatoes and brown them on all sides, turning them often with a spatula. This is tedious but takes only 10 minutes.

❈ Add the onion and pepper and cook until the onion is translucent. Add the chicken, gravy, and salt and pepper to taste. Toss with a spoon or spatula until everything is coated with gravy.

❈ Cover and simmer for 5 to 7 minutes (but don't let the bottom burn)!

Serves 4

Chicken with Clementines & Fennel

The marinade sits for an hour, or overnight, your choice. Don't peel the clementines!

6 tablespoons brandy

4 tablespoons olive oil

3 tablespoons orange juice

3 tablespoons lemon juice

2 tablespoons grainy mustard

3 tablespoons brown sugar

I teaspoon cumin

I tablespoon fresh thyme

I½ teaspoons sea salt

Freshly ground pepper

2 large chicken breasts (or I whole chicken) cut into 8 pieces.

I large or two small fennel pounds, cut into quarters

4 clementines, UNPEELED and sliced into thin slices

I tablespoon fresh thyme

I cup vegetable broth

Parsley to garnish

❋ In a large bowl, whisk together the brandy, olive oil, OJ, lemon juice, mustard, brown sugar, cumin, thyme, salt, and pepper. Add the chicken, fennel, and clementines.

❋ Marinate for an hour, or overnight.

❋ Put everything into a roasting pan, tucking fennel and clementines next to the chicken pieces. Pour the vegetable broth around the edges.

❋ Bake at 450 degrees for 35 to 45 minutes, until the chicken is browned.

❋ Arrange the chicken and fennel and clementines on a platter.

❋ Pour the sauce into a sauce pan and reduce to 1 cup over medium high heat, watching and stirring.

❋ Pour it over the chicken, fennel, and clementines on the platter. Garnish with parsley.

Serves 4

Leftovers: The leftover chicken, chopped clementines, and fennel makes a terrific chicken salad.

Chicken with Sweet Potatoes & Artichoke Hearts

Be sure to consider the leftovers, described at the end of the recipe.

2 pounds bone-in chicken breasts

1/2 cup olive oil

Salt and pepper

1 jar or can of artichoke hearts

2 medium sweet potatoes, cut into 1-inch pieces

1 small yellow onion, peeled and chopped

1 garlic clove, minced

1 lemon zested, plus 2 tablespoons lemon juice

1 tablespoon Dijon mustard

1 small yellow onion, peeled and chopped

2 cups chicken stock or vegetable stock

1 teaspoon cinnamon

1/2 teaspoon cumin

Parsley, chopped, to serve

❋ Heat oven to 425 degrees.

❋ In a large bowl, toss the chicken with the olive oil, salt, and pepper. Place chicken in a 10- to 12-inch cast-iron fry pan.

❋ In the same bowl you used for the chicken, toss the artichokes, sweet potatoes, onion, garlic, lemon zest, lemon juice, and mustard. Add to chicken, tucking artichokes in between the chicken breasts.

❋ Pour 2 cups of chicken stock or vegetable stock over everything.

❋ Roast for 35 to 45 minutes, until the chicken and potatoes are nicely browned.

❋ Sprinkle the cinnamon and cumin over the top, and then carefully spoon the sauce over the chicken.

❋ Serve with parsley sprinkled on top.

Now for the best part: leftovers!

Serves 4

Leftovers: Save the chicken for chicken salad or chicken noodle soup. But the sauce with the artichokes makes the best cream of artichoke soup!

Cream of Artichoke Soup: Put the leftover sauce in a blender with a cup of coconut milk (or other milk of your choice) and a cup of vegetable broth. Then whiz it up.

Serve hot with almost any herb sprinkled on top: parsley or oregano or dill or chives.

Duck à l'Orange

This is the first duck recipe I ever tried. It comes – via my cousin Carol Ann – from La Toque Blanche, a French restaurant in New York City (now closed). If you have a game bird, this is not the recipe!

1 plump Long Island duckling (about 6–7 pounds)

FOR THE SAUCE

2 navel oranges

2 tablespoons sugar

2 tablespoons red wine vinegar

3 cubes beef bouillon

2 tablespoons red currant jelly

1 tablespoon cornstarch, mixed with 1 tablespoon water

Salt and pepper

❊ Preheat the oven to 425°F.

❊ Wash the duck and roast it on a rack in a high-sided roasting pan for 3 hours. Check the pan often and pour off the fat as it accumulates (I keep clean coffee cans for this). When it is crispy and brown, it is done.

❊ Peel the zest off the oranges into thin slivers. Cut the orange pulp into chunks.

❊ While the duck is cooking, make the sauce. In a small saucepan, combine the orange zest with 1 cup water. Boil for 10 minutes. Drain the liquid off and set aside.

❊ In a saucepan combine the orange pulp and sugar over medium heat. Bring to a boil and boil for 10 minutes. Add the vinegar and bouillon cubes. Using a wooden spoon, break up the cubes until they are mixed in.

❊ Continue boiling until the mixture is reduced by half. Strain and return the mixture to the heat.

❊ Add the currant jelly and thicken with the cornstarch mixture. Stir in the reserved orange zest.

❊ Transfer the duck to a cutting board and let it cool for 10 minutes, Cut it into 4 large pieces, starting down the backbone and breast bone and then across under the breast. I use heavy kitchen scissors.

❊ Serve it with the orange sauce in a bowl on the side.

Serves 4

Duck Breasts Marsala

This recipe is for a game bird, not a fat Long Island duckling. A friend of mine who hunts recently handed me a warm, recently shot mallard hen. I tried to imagine plucking it so I could roast it, but it was small. The only real meat was the breast. I cut the breasts out so there were two small pieces of duck without bones or skin.

2 duck breast medallions

1/4 cup flour

2 tablespoons butter

2 tablespoons chopped sweet
onion or scallions

1/4 cup Marsala wine

1 tablespoon heavy cream

❋ Rinse the duck breasts in cold water and dredge them in the flour.

❋ In a cast-iron skillet, heat the butter over medium heat. When it is sizzling add the duck breasts and brown them quickly, 3 minutes per side. Transfer the duck to a warm platter.

❋ Add the onions to the skillet and cook until translucent. Add the wine and let it boil 1 minute. Add the cream and salt and pepper to taste.

❋ Return the duck to the pan for 3 minutes to reheat and coat it with sauce.

Serves 2

Cassoulet

This is a casserole of leftover duck, pork, goose, turkey, and sausage cooked slowly in white beans. It's a hearty, filling, winter dish, perfect for the ski season and generally served after Christmas when you might have all those leftovers (save all of the gravy). Served with a loaf of country bread and a big salad, this is a great meal. For the pork, you can use a kielbasa sausage. Instead of turkey, you can use chicken.

1 bag great northern white beans

1 large onion, chopped

Leaves from 2 sprigs fresh sage or 2 teaspoons dried sage

Salt and pepper

4 cups water

4 cups chicken stock

2 cups gravy from the leftovers

3 or 4 pieces cooked duck or goose

6 to 8 pieces cooked turkey or chicken

6 slices pork, or a kielbasa sausage, cooked and sliced

❇ Rinse the beans and place in a large, heavy pot. Cover the beans with water until the water is 1 inch over the top of the beans.

❇ Add the onion, sage, and salt and pepper to taste. Bring to a boil.

❇ Lower the heat and simmer for 3 hours. As the water level drops, add the chicken stock, 1 cup at a time.

❇ Preheat the oven to 275°F.

❇ When the beans are almost done, add the gravies and the meats. Cover and bake for 30 to 45 minutes, until the meats are hot and the beans fully cooked.

Serves 8

Roast Tenderloin of Beef with Wild Mushroom Sauce

These long thin roasts are the tender, delicious cut of beef, but also the most expensive – they are perfect for a dinner party. Allow one-third pound of meat per person. You can also grill the meat, but if you do, be sure to coat it with some olive oil and ground pepper.

The creamy wild mushroom sauce is a terrific accompaniment. Fresh morels, chanterelles, or porcini (also known as boletes) work very well. If these are not available, you can use standard white mushrooms, and may add some dried morels, chanterelles and/or porcini to them.

If you're not a mushroom lover, serve with Hollandaise Sauce (page 94) instead.

FOR THE MEAT

2 pounds beef tenderloin

Salt and pepper

FOR THE SAUCE

4 tablespoons (1/2 stick) butter

1 pound mushrooms, washed and sliced thin

2 cloves garlic, minced

2 tablespoons Cognac or applejack

1/4 teaspoon dried thyme or sage

Salt and pepper

1/2 cup heavy cream

❄ Preheat the oven to 400°F.

❄ Wash and dry the tenderloin. Place it in a roasting pan and season with salt and pepper. Let the meat come to room temperature before cooking.

❄ For perfect medium-rare meat, roast for 45 minutes. Let it cool on the cutting board for 10 minutes before slicing it.

❄ **To make the sauce:** In a cast-iron skillet, melt the butter over medium heat. Add the mushrooms and sauté until they have released their liquid. Add the garlic and sauté for 2 minutes. Stir in the Cognac and let it boil away.

❄ Lower the heat and stir in the thyme, cream, and salt and pepper to taste. Cook the sauce until it thickens – about 4 minutes. Transfer to a bowl for serving.

If you use dried mushrooms, soak them in warm water for 5 minutes before using them.

Serves 6–8

Beef Stroganoff

My sister, Cindy, taught me this recipe before I went to cooking school. You could say that it's the first thing I learned how to cook. Thank you, Cindy! You will need 1 slice of cooked roast beef per person (you can use leftover roast beef, if you have it). Serve over fairly large flat noodles.

8 slices cooked roast beef
(or 2 pounds top round)

2 tablespoons butter

1 large onion, chopped

8 ounces fresh button mushrooms,
sliced (or use canned ones)

1 cup leftover gravy (or beef broth
with 2 tablespoons flour)

1/2 cup sour cream

2 tablespoons tomato paste

1 tablespoon Worcestershire
sauce

Dash of Tabasco

Salt and pepper

❅ Cut the beef into thin strips the size of a finger. If you are using uncooked meat, dredge the strips in 3 tablespoons of flour and brown them in 1 tablespoon of butter.

❅ In a cast-iron skillet, melt the butter over medium heat. Add the onion and sauté until it is translucent. Add the mushrooms and sauté for 3 minutes. Add the beef and gravy. Simmer for 5 minutes.

❅ In a bowl, stir together the sour cream, tomato paste, Worcestershire sauce, and Tabasco. Stir this mixture into the skillet. Add salt and pepper to taste, and simmer for 10 minutes while you cook the noodles.

Serves 4

Roast Beef Hash

This is definitely a good dish to use up leftovers. You can serve it for breakfast with a poached egg on top, or as a lunch with rolls and salad.

2 tablespoons butter

2 baking potatoes cut into smallest cubes possible

I large onion, minced

I green bell pepper, minced

2 cups cubed cooked roast beef, cut as small as possible

1/2 cup leftover gravy

I teaspoon dried thyme

Salt and pepper

❋ In a cast-iron skillet, melt the butter over medium heat. Add the potatoes and brown them, flipping them with a spatula for 10 minutes to brown all sides.

❋ Add the onion and green pepper and cook until the onion is translucent. Add the beef, gravy, thyme, and salt and pepper to taste. Cook over low heat for 5 to 10 minutes until the mixture is heated through and comes together like hash.

❋ Serve out of the skillet or transfer to a warm bowl.

Serves 6–8

Use Mock Gravy (page 89) if you don't have leftover gravy.

Early morning coffee with Diablo

Dijon & Brandy Beef Stew

This is the best beef stew I ever tasted! The mustard and Brandy give the stew a pleasant spiciness, and the mushrooms give it richness. You can use a mixture of mushrooms, and you can use Dijon mustard if you don't have the Pommery mustard.

1/4 pound salt pork
or thick bacon diced

I large onion chopped

3 shallots peeled and chopped

4 tablespoons butter

2 pounds beef,
cut into 1-inch cubes

2 tablespoons flour

1/2 cup brandy

2 tablespoons
Pommery mustard (or Dijon)

2 cups beef stock or chicken stock

4 large carrots, peeled and cut
into half-moon slices

1/2 pound mushrooms, cut in
quarters.

1/4 cup red wine

❋ In a heavy stew pot, cook the salt pork or bacon until fat is rendered. Discard the pork and cook the onion and shallots until soft.

❋ Put the cooked onions and shallots into a large bowl.

❋ In a separate bowl, toss beef cubes in flour, to coat.

❋ Add half the butter to the pot and brown the flour-coated beef cubes. Add beef to the bowl with the onions and shallots.

❋ Add brandy to the pot and scrape the bottom for the browned pieces of flour. Add the beef stock or chicken stock to the pot. Add the mustard and whisk until everything is blended.

❋ Add the beef and onion to the pot and cover.

❋ Simmer for 90 minutes.

❋ Add the carrots and simmer for another 30 minutes.

❋ Meanwhile, sauté the mushrooms in a skillet with the remaining butter until brown. Add the mushrooms to the pot.

❋ Add the red wine and simmer 5 minutes.

❋ Taste and correct seasoning.

Serves 6–8

Jim's St. Patrick's Day Dinner

I corned beef brisket

Olive oil or butter to sauté onions

2 large yellow onions, cut into
large chunks

4 large carrots, sliced

4 baking potatoes, peeled and cut
into big chunks

I head of cabbage, cut
into quarters

I tablespoon cloves

Salt and pepper

2 quarts water

Horseradish, to serve

White vinegar, to serve

❄ In a very large pot (4- to 6-quart size), sauté the onions for 2 minutes. Add the corned beef and carrots, salt and pepper, cloves, and water and bring to a boil. Lower to just barely bubbling, then cover the pot and simmer for 4 hours.

❄ Add the potatoes and bring it up to a boil, cook for 20 minutes. Add the cabbage and boil for an additional 30 minutes, until a sharp knife pushes into the cabbage easily.

❄ Slice the corned beef, and arrange it on a large platter, surrounding it with the vegetables.

❄ Serve with horseradish and mustard for the beef, and white vinegar in a small pitcher for the cabbage.

Serves 8

Hungarian Goulash

Don't try this unless you have Hungarian paprika, which is much stronger and tastier than regular paprika. The Hungarian freedom fighter that I learned this from would die to hear that I use leftover roast beef, but it works very well. Hungarians use raw beef (top round). Serve this with a loaf of whole wheat bread.

I cup cooked beef
(or uncooked top round) cut into
bite-size pieces

2 tablespoons butter

I large onion, chopped

2 cloves garlic, chopped

2 tablespoons Hungarian paprika

1/4 cup white wine

2 cups water

1/4 cup sour cream

I tablespoon Worcestershire sauce

❊ If you use raw beef, first dredge the pieces in 3 tablespoons of flour and brown in 1 tablespoon of butter in a cast-iron skillet.

❊ In a soup pot, melt the butter over medium heat. Add the onion and garlic and cook until browned. Add the paprika and stir it around; the butter brings out the taste.

❊ Add the wine and let it boil until almost all is absorbed.

❊ Add the beef and water. Simmer for 1 hour.

❊ Stir in the sour cream and Worcestershire sauce. Taste and add salt and pepper if necessary.

Serves 4

Charred Vietnamese Flank Steak

This is not really "camp cooking," but it is so delicious I thought I would include it. Flank steak is a flavorful cut of meat that is relatively inexpensive. It requires marinating before cooking and is delicious served medium-rare. You can substitute regular basil for the Thai variety here. If you want to do it camp style, use the marinade for chicken on page 155.

FOR THE MARINADE

2 tablespoons chopped garlic (about 6 cloves)

1/4 cup minced fresh ginger

4 large jalapeño peppers, seeded and minced

2/3 cup sugar

2 teaspoons red chili paste

1 cup fish sauce (available in the Asian section of most supermarkets)

Zest and juice of 6 large limes

2 teaspoons ground coriander

FOR THE MEAT

2 pounds flank steak, fat trimmed

1/4 cup chopped fresh coriander

1/4 cup chopped fresh Thai basil

1 small head iceberg lettuce, leaves separated

Coriander sprigs

Thai basil sprigs

❋ Combine all the marinade ingredients in a medium bowl.

❋ Put the steak into a gallon-size resealable plastic bag, pour in the marinade, and let the steak marinate for at least 3 hours or overnight in the refrigerator. Bring the steak to room temperature prior to cooking.

❋ Preheat a gas grill to high heat.

❋ Remove the steak from the marinade and sprinkle both sides with the chopped coriander and basil. Grill the steak for 4 to 6 minutes per side or until medium-rare. Transfer the steak to a cutting board and let it rest for 5 minutes.

❋ Strain the marinade into a small saucepan. Place over high heat and bring to a boil. Let it boil for 3 minutes. Remove from the heat and let it cool.

❋ Cut the steak across the grain into thin slices and serve with lettuce leaves and herb sprigs. To eat, wrap 3 slices of steak and 2 herb sprigs in a lettuce leaf and dip it in the sauce.

Serves 4–6

 # LAMB

Lamb Stew

This classic Irish stew is traditionally served with a very thin sauce. The Irish used older sheep — mutton — and cooked it for hours to tenderize it. The best cut for this recipe is the lamb shank. I also prefer a thicker sauce.

3 pounds lamb (4 shanks)

I large firm (Idaho) potato, peeled and cut into chunks

I large onion, sliced

3 red potatoes, sliced (these dissolve during the cooking and thicken the sauce)

2 bay leaves

1/2 teaspoon dried thyme

1/2 teaspoon dried oregano

Salt and pepper

❋ Preheat the oven to 350°F.

❋ Cut the meat off the lamb shanks, then cut it into 1-inch chunks.

❋ In an ovenproof dish about the size of a small lasagna dish (7 x 9 inches) layer the ingredients as follows: Idaho potatoes, onion, lamb, red potatoes, onion, lamb, and red potatoes.

❋ Tuck the bay leaves into the casserole. Season with the thyme, oregano, and salt and pepper to taste.

❋ Pour water in to reach the top of the dish. Cover with a good lid or tin foil.

❋ Bake for 3 hours, or until potatoes have dissolved and made the gravy thick.

Serves 6–8

Lamb Kebobs

This is a really good recipe when you have some guests who love lamb and others who don't particularly like it. The marinade takes the "gaminess" out of the lamb.

FOR THE MARINADE

1/2 cup tarragon vinegar

1/2 cup dry sherry

1 large onion, sliced

Salt

8 peppercorns

1 bay leaf

2 cloves garlic, crushed

FOR THE KEBOBS

4 lamb shanks or 2 pounds
boneless lamb

2 green bell peppers,
cut into chunks

1 basket cherry tomatoes

2 medium sweet onions (Vidalia,
Maui or red), cut into chunks

❊ Cut the meat off the lamb shanks, then cut it into 2-inch chunks.

❊ In a saucepan, bring all the marinade ingredients to a boil. Remove from the heat and let cool.

❊ Place the lamb chunks in a bowl and pour the cooled marinade over them. Cover with plastic wrap and refrigerate overnight.

❊ Put the lamb chunks onto skewers, alternating with the peppers, onion, and tomatoes.

❊ Preheat a gas grill to high.

❊ Grill the kebobs for 7 minutes a side. Serve on a pretty platter with skewers removed.

Serves 4

Shepherd's Pie

This is almost better than a roast leg of lamb, and it's a good reason for making plenty of mashed potatoes.

I tablespoon butter

I large onion, chopped

I green bell pepper, chopped

4 cups cooked lamb, cut into tiny pieces

1/2 cup gravy

Salt and pepper

1½ to 2 cups mashed potatoes

❋ Preheat the oven to 350°F.

❋ In a cast-iron skillet melt the butter over medium heat. Add the onion and cook until it is translucent. Add the green pepper and cook until softened. Add the lamb, gravy, and salt and pepper to taste. Cook until it bubbles.

❋ Transfer the mixture to a baking dish or large pie dish. Spread the mashed potatoes on top.

❋ Bake for 30 minutes or until the potato crust is brown at the edges and the pie is bubbling.

Serves 4

Grilled Leg of Lamb

No one can tell what game meat this is when we serve it. It tastes like elk or buffalo. Because it is boned and marinated, it grills like a steak. I like to serve it with Potatoes Dauphinoise (page 145).

8-pound leg of lamb, boned and split

FOR THE MARINADE

I cup molasses

I cup soy sauce

6 cloves garlic, minced

❋ Combine the molasses, soy sauce, and garlic.

❋ Place the lamb in a large glass lasagna dish and pour the marinade over it. Marinate for 3 to 24 hours.

❋ Grill or broil the lamb just as you would a steak – about 7 minutes a side. Cut into slices and serve on a warm platter.

Serves 8–10

Moussaka

This is a yummy Greek dish made with layered eggplant, lamb, and cream sauce. You can make it a day ahead, which makes it even tastier.

FOR THE LAMB

2 tablespoons butter

1 onion, chopped

1 green bell pepper, chopped

2 cups cooked lamb cut into tiny pieces (you can use ground lamb cooked in butter)

Dash of cumin

Salt and pepper

FOR THE SAUCE

2 tablespoons butter

2 tablespoons flour

2 cups half-and-half

Nutmeg

FOR THE EGGPLANT

1 eggplant, peeled and cut into 1/4-inch slices

❋ **To prepare the lamb:** In a cast-iron skillet melt the butter over medium heat. Add the onion and green pepper and sauté until the onion is translucent. Add the lamb, cumin, and salt and pepper to taste. Remove from heat and set aside.

❋ **To make the sauce:** Melt the butter in a saucepan. Add the flour and stir as it balls up. Add the half-and-half and whisk it until it is smooth and very thick. Stir in the nutmeg.

❋ **To prepare the eggplant:** Preheat the broiler. Broil the eggplant slices for 5 minutes per side.

❋ Preheat the oven to 350°F. Butter a 7 x 9-inch lasagna dish.

❋ **To assemble the moussaka:** Start with a layer of eggplant, then a layer of lamb, then a layer of cream sauce. Repeat with remaining ingredients. The last layer should be cream sauce.

❋ Bake for 40 minutes or until it bubbles.

Serves 6

Lamb Curry

A friend of mine, Pawan Mehra, an excellent Indian chef, tells me that there is no curry powder (as such) in India. To Indians, curry literally means "sauce." Curry powder was invented by the British, who wanted a standard spice mix for Indian food. True Indian curries begin with sautéed caramelized onion, coriander, and cumin. This makes for a very mild and basic curry. All of my curries start with sautéed onion and apple. I then add curry powder, which must be cooked. You can add hot pepper, fenugreek, mace, nutmeg and/or ginger, depending on your taste.

2 tablespoons butter

1 onion, chopped

1 stalk celery, chopped

1 apple, peeled and chopped

1 tablespoon flour

1 tablespoon curry powder

1 cup chicken stock or 1/2 cup stock and 1/2 cup coconut milk

2 cups cooked lamb, cut into small pieces

1 teaspoon grated lemon zest

Dash of nutmeg

Salt and lots of black pepper

Rice (page 84)

CONDIMENTS

1/2 cup raisins

1/2 cup coconut flakes

1/2 cup peanuts, chopped

1 cup chutney (Major Grey, Bengal hot, or Peach Chutney (page 226)

1 cup sour cream

1 avocado, sliced

❄ In a cast-iron skillet, melt the butter over medium heat. Add the onion and celery and sauté for 5 minutes.

❄ Add the apple and cook for 5 minutes.

❄ Add the flour and curry powder and stir it around so the curry powder is cooked in the butter to remove any bitter flavor.

❄ Add the chicken stock and stir to combine.

❄ Add the lamb. Cover and simmer for 20 minutes. Add the lemon zest, nutmeg, and salt and pepper. Serve with rice and the condiments on the side.

Serves 4

Variation: For **shrimp curry**, substitute 2 cups of cooked shrimp for the lamb and follow the recipe.

Note: For yellow curries, add turmeric. For red curries, add Kashmiri paprika and turmeric (smoked Kashmiri paprika is especially flavorful). Fenugreek is an especially effective ingredient. Today, many Indian spices are available at high-end supermarkets or you can buy them on the internet from sources such as spicehunter.com or penzeys.com

Lamb Meatballs

This could also be made into a meatloaf, or used in a pasta sauce. See notes at end of recipe. Do not use a glass bowl when preparing this dish!

1 pound ground lamb

1 small onion, chopped

2 cloves garlic, minced

1 large hot, red chili, seeded and chopped (use gloves!)

1 teaspoon cinnamon

1 teaspoon Old Bay spice or allspice

3/4 tsp nutmeg

Salt and pepper

1/4 cup chopped parsley

1 egg

1/2 cup bread crumbs

Large can of V8 juice

3 tablespoons pine nuts, for garnish

1 tablespoon chopped parsley, for garnish

❈ Mix all of above, except the V8 and the garnish ingredients, in large metal or wooden bowl, as if you were making a meat loaf.

❈ When it is mixed, make one big ball and raise it up and then slam it down hard into the bowl to activate the glutens. Do this 3 or 4 times, until the ball stays together.

❈ Now make meat balls about the size of a golf ball or ping-pong ball, and set them aside on a plate.

❈ Pour enough V8 juice into a large caste-iron pan so it goes halfway up the sides. Heat this up to not-quite boiling.

❈ Put the meat balls into the pan and poach them on low heat, so the liquid is gently bubbling, NOT at a roiling boil (which will cause the balls to separate into mush). Every 10 minutes or so, roll the balls a bit in order to eventually cook all sides.

❈ When done, put the balls in a nice flat dish with sides and pour the juice in. Serve with pine nuts and chopped parsley on top.

Serves 4
(or serves lots more people, if you are serving as an appetizer)

If the balls turn to mush, do not despair! Add marinara sauce and serve it as a spaghetti sauce. Or make the tomato sauce into shakshuka sauce, and serve the lamb with it on top of grilled eggplant slices.

PORK

Pork Chops with Glazed Apples

This is true comfort food, especially on a cool fall or winter night.

6 pork chops, 1-inch thick

FOR THE MARINADE

1/2 cup soy sauce

1/2 cup olive oil

1/4 cup balsamic vinegar

2 cloves garlic, crushed

Leaves from 2 sprigs of sage, rosemary, or thyme

FOR THE APPLES

2 teaspoons grated orange zest

1/2 cup orange juice

1/2 cup white wine vinegar

4 red apples, cored and quartered, unpeeled

❄ Whisk together the soy sauce, olive oil, vinegar, garlic, and sage.

❄ Put the pork chops in a resealable plastic bag. Pour the marinade into the bag and refrigerate for 3 hours.

❄ In a cast-iron skillet, combine the orange zest, orange juice, and vinegar. Arrange the apples on top, skin side up.

❄ Cover and cook for 10 to 15 minutes.

❄ Preheat the grill or broiler.

❄ Grill or broil the pork chops for 7 minutes per side. Transfer the chops to a platter.

❄ Transfer the apples to the platter around the grilled pork chops. Let the juice in the skillet boil down until thickened. Spoon it over the apples.

Serves 6

Grilled Pork Tenderloin

We make this often in the summer and serve it with baked apples or homemade applesauce.

2 pork tenderloins

Fresh parsley, for garnish

FOR THE MARINADE

6 cloves garlic, finely chopped

1/2 cup thick teriyaki sauce

1/4 cup olive oil

1/4 cup dark molasses

2 tablespoons red wine vinegar

1 tablespoon coarsely ground
black pepper

1 teaspoon salt

1 teaspoon dried or fresh oregano

1 teaspoon dried or 1 tablespoon
fresh rosemary, crushed
or finely chopped

2 tablespoons Louisiana hot sauce
(optional)

❈ Rinse the tenderloins in cold water and pat dry on paper towels. Place them in a gallon-size resealable plastic bag.

❈ Add the marinade ingredients. Seal the bag and shake, rattle, and roll until all of the ingredients are thoroughly mixed and the tenderloins are completely coated. Open the bag slightly and release the excess air by squeezing the bag. Reseal.

❈ Place the bag on a platter and let it sit for at least 2 hours at room temperature. (This may be made up a day or two in advance and kept in the refrigerator. Let stand for 1 hour before cooking.)

❈ Preheat the grill or broiler to hot.

❈ Remove the tenderloins from the bag with tongs and place on the platter. Pour the extra marinade into a small saucepan. Discard the bag.

❈ Bring the marinade to a boil and boil for 3 minutes. Set aside.

❈ Grill the pork for 5 minutes on each of 3 sides for 15 minutes total (pretend that the tenderloins are triangular).

❈ Spoon the reserved marinade on each of the just-cooked sides for more flavor and moisture.

❈ Transfer the pork to a cutting board, and let rest for 3 minutes. Cut into 1/2- to 3/4-inch-thick slices.

❈ Arrange the slices on a platter, pour the juices from the board over the top, and garnish with fresh parsley.

Serves 6

Ham Hash

I have often thought that the definition of infinity is two people stuck with one ham after a dinner party. Ham hash is an excellent antidote, and a great use of leftover ham. If you don't have leftover ham, you may use canned ham.

I tablespoon butter

I potato, peeled and cut into small cubes

I onion, chopped

I cup very small ham cubes

I green bell pepper, chopped

I dill pickle, chopped

I tablespoon pickle juice

I tablespoon Worcestershire sauce

I teaspoon dried thyme

Salt and pepper

❋ In a cast-iron skillet, melt the butter over medium heat. Add the potato and brown for 11 minutes.

❋ Add the onion and cook until it is translucent.

❋ Add the green pepper and stir for 2 minutes.

❋ Add the ham, pickle, pickle juice, Worcestershire, thyme, and salt and pepper to taste.

❋ Cover and cook over low heat for 5 minutes until everything is hot and the juices have evaporated. If it looks like hash, it is!

Serves 4

Eggs Benedict

This is a great brunch dish. The hardest part of this assembly is having it all hot when you serve it, so follow the directions carefully.

Hollandaise Sauce (page 94)

4 English muffins

8 thin slices of ham (a slice on each toasted muffin half)

8 eggs

❋ Make the Hollandaise first.

❋ Toast the English muffins. Put 2 English muffin halves on each plate. Put a slice of ham on each muffin.

❋ Poach the eggs for 1 minute in boiling water. Put an egg on each muffin. Top with spoonful of Hollandaise.

Serves 4

VEAL

Today I find veal on many menus because it is light, low in cholesterol, and easily adaptable to many flavors. Veal can be found in most modern supermarkets or at your local butcher. If you have an objection to veal, chicken breasts or pork cutlets can be substituted in the schnitzel and marsala recipes. If you can't find veal in the regular meat department, look in the frozen foods section.

Osso Buco

This is a traditional Italian dish made with veal shanks that are cooked very slowly (braised). You can ask your butcher for them. This recipe can also be used for lamb shanks.

4 veal shanks

Flour for dredging

2 strips bacon

1 large onion, chopped

1 cup white wine

Leaves from 1 sprig rosemary

1/4 cup heavy cream

Salt and pepper

Chopped parsley, for garnish

❊ Rinse and dry the shanks. Then dredge them in flour.

❊ Chop the bacon into little bits and fry it in a tall heavy pot. Add the shanks and brown them over fairly high heat for 10 minutes, turning them often

❊ Add the onion and cook until translucent. Add the wine and let it boil off a little. Add the rosemary, and salt and pepper to taste. Lower the heat as much as possible, and cover the pot with a tight lid.

❊ Cook very slowly for 3 hours.

❊ Transfer the veal shanks to a platter. Continue to cook the juices in the pot until they thicken. Whisk in the cream and more salt and pepper if necessary. Pour the sauce over the veal and garnish with chopped parsley.

Serves 4

Variation: For **braised lamb shanks**, follow this recipe, omitting the cream.

Wiener Schnitzel with Wine & Caper Sauce

When I was 12 or 13, I worked on Granddaddy's dairy farm in Upper Jay, New York, helping to harvest the hay. There were 45 herefords and one bull. Bull calves were sold when they were a week old for veal. This was a harsh reality for a 12-year-old, and I refused to eat veal for many years until I was on my honeymoon in Germany, where veal is a countrywide specialty. You can find veal schnitzel prepared a hundred ways in that part of the world. The Germans do veal as many different ways as the Italians do pasta. Here's a classic Wiener Schnitzel, which is veal that is dipped in eggs, breaded, and fried. If you don't want to make the sauce, just serve with lemon wedges.

FOR THE VEAL

8 veal scallops, pounded thin

2 eggs beaten with 1/3 cup milk

Flour for dredging

4 tablespoons (1/2 stick) butter

1 tablespoon vegetable oil

FOR THE SAUCE

1 medium onion, chopped

1/2 cup white wine

2 teaspoons capers

1/2 teaspoon salt

1 teaspoon pepper

1 teaspoon lemon juice

1/4 cup heavy cream

❋ If you buy the veal scallops thick and unpounded, rinse them and place on a clean dish towel or between two pieces of waxed paper. Fold the end of the towel over the top so that the meat is completely covered on both sides, with enough overhang to accommodate the larger flattened scallop.

❋ Pound the meat with a rolling pin or meat hammer, 20 to 25 good whacks for each piece should do it.

❋ Dip each veal scallop in the egg and milk mixture, saturating it thoroughly, and then dredge with flour so that each side is dusted. You may add salt, pepper, or spices to the flour if you like.

❋ Heat the butter and oil in a cast-iron skillet over medium heat. When the butter and oil are bubbling, put 2 to 3 scallops in the pan and fry for 3 minutes, turn, and fry the other side for 3 minutes.

❋ Transfer to a warm platter. Repeat with the remaining veal.

❋ **To make the sauce:** In the skillet, sauté the onion for 5 minutes. Add the wine and let it boil off a little. Add the capers, salt, pepper, and lemon juice. Stir in the cream.

Serves 4

Veal Piccata

Veal picatta is the classic choice. The whole dish can be completed in 30 minutes. The juices from the veal combine with the wine, butter, and lemon to make a delicate, tangy sauce. Served with good fresh bread and a tossed salad, you can have an impressive and delicious meal in less than an hour — and that includes setting the table and lighting the candles!

8 veal scallops, pounded thin

Flour for dredging

4 to 6 tablespoons butter

2 small onions or 1 large onion, chopped

1/2 cup white wine or champagne

1 cup chicken stock

Juice of 2 lemons

Capers, for garnish

Salt and pepper

❈ If you buy the veal scallops thick and unpounded, rinse them and place on a clean dish towel or between two pieces of waxed paper. Fold the end of the towel or paper so that the meat is completely covered on both sides with enough over-hang to accommodate the larger flattened scallop.

❈ Pound the meat with a rolling pin or meat hammer, 20 to 25 whacks for each piece should do it. Dredge the veal in flour.

❈ Melt the butter in a cast-iron skillet with a tight lid or a sauté pan (which is like the skillet with straight 3-inch-high sides).

❈ Add 2 to 3 veal scallops and sauté until brown, 3 minutes per side.

❈ Transfer to a warm platter. Repeat with the remaining veal.

❈ Add the onion to the skillet and sauté until translucent.

❈ Add the wine and let it boil 1 minute. Add the chicken stock and cook for 5 minutes.

❈ Continue cooking the sauce until it thickens. Add the lemon juice, capers, and salt and pepper to taste.

❈ Plate, and pour the sauce over the veal.

Serves 4

Veal Marsala

This recipe is similar to veal piccata, but it has a cream sauce.

8 veal scallops, pounded thin

Flour for dredging

4 to 6 tablespoons butter

1/2 cup Marsala
or good cream sherry

1 cup chicken stock

1/4 cup heavy cream

Dash nutmeg

Salt and pepper

❋ If you buy the veal scallops thick and unpounded, rinse them and place on a clean dish towel or between two pieces of waxed paper. Fold the end of the towel or paper so that the meat is completely covered on both sides with enough overhang to accommodate the larger flattened scallop.

❋ Pound the meat with a rolling pin or meat hammer, 20 to 25 whacks for each piece should do it. Dredge the veal in flour.

❋ Melt the butter in a cast-iron skillet with a tight lid or a sauté pan (which is like the skillet with straight 3-inch-high sides).

❋ Add 2 to 3 veal scallops and sauté until brown, 3 minutes per side.

❋ Transfer to a warm platter.

❋ Repeat with the remaining veal.

❋ Add the wine to the skillet and let it boil 1 minute. Add the chicken stock and cook for 5 minutes.

❋ Continue cooking the sauce until it thickens. Add the cream, nutmeg, and salt and pepper to taste.

❋ Plate, and pour the sauce over the veal.

Serves 4

Veal Stew

A great recipe for a cool fall night, this can be scaled for any number of guests. You can make this recipe with beef instead, but veal is lighter in flavor.

I pound veal cubes (cut from veal roast or veal chops)

Flour for dredging

4 tablespoons butter

I large red onion, chopped

2 stalks celery, chopped

I leek sliced thin (soak the slices in water for 10 minutes)

I cup white wine

2 cups chicken stock

Leaves from 3 sprigs thyme

I rutabaga, peeled and cut into 1-inch cubes

10 baby carrots

2 potatoes, peeled and cut into cubes

Salt and pepper

Chopped parsley, for garnish

❊ Rinse the veal and it pat dry with a towel. Dredge the veal in flour.

❊ In large soup pot, melt 2 tablespoons of the butter over medium heat. Add 6 to 8 pieces of veal at a time and brown them on all sides, about 4 minutes.

❊ Transfer the browned pieces to a plate and brown another batch until all the veal is cooked, using the remaining 2 tablespoons of butter as needed. (Don't try to brown all the veal at once; it will stick together and be mushy.)

❊ Add the onion, celery, and leek to the pot and cook until soft. Add the wine and let it boil off a bit. Add the chicken stock and return the veal to the pot. Add the thyme, reduce the heat to low and simmer for 2 hours.

❊ Add the rutabaga, carrots, and potato and bring to a slow boil. Let boil for 20 minutes.

❊ Now it's ready! Taste it and add salt and pepper. Sprinkle chopped parsley on top.

Serves 4

Veal Loaf

My friend Sheila Rosenblatt gave me this recipe. It's a great summer lunch. You can make it ahead and keep it in the refrigerator. It should be served cold with a tossed salad and a loaf of good bread. I usually serve a bowl of ranch dressing on the side.

1½ pounds ground veal

1/2 pound ground beef

1 medium onion, chopped

1/4 cup breadcrumbs

1 egg

Salt and pepper

1/4 teaspoon curry powder

1 bunch watercress, most of stems cut off

❈ Preheat the oven to 350°F.

❈ In a large wooden salad bowl, mix together all the ingredients except the watercress. Use your hands to form a ball. Throw it hard into the bowl about 4 times (this is why you want to use a salad bowl and not a glass one). The throwing activates the glutens so the meat stays together.

❈ Flatten the ball on a board. Place the watercress on the left side and roll the meat around it so that the watercress is in the center. Put into a loaf pan.

❈ Bake for 2 hours. Let the loaf cool before removing it from the pan and slicing.

Each slice will have a pretty, green, watercress center.

Serves 6–8

FISH & SEAFOOD

Trout Amandine

Keene Valley has a world-class fishing river, the Ausable, running through it. In the winter, we live in Sun Valley, Idaho, where we have lots of yummy Idaho trout. As a result, we don't go too many days without eating this wonderful, freshwater fish.

4 tablespoons (1/2 stick) butter

1 trout large enough for 2 people
(12 to 14 inches)

Flour for dredging

2 cloves garlic, minced

1/2 cup slivered almonds

1 tablespoon lemon juice

Salt and pepper

Parsley or chopped chives,
for garnish

❋ Rinse the trout and pat it dry. Dredge it in the flour, and shake off the excess.

❋ Melt the butter in a sauté pan over medium heat. Add the trout to the pan and cook on one side until it is brown, about 8 minutes.

❋ Turn it and cook the second side for 6 to 7 minutes spooning butter into the open belly cavity. Transfer it to a warm platter.

❋ Add the garlic to the pan and sauté for 2 minutes. Add the almonds, lemon juice, and salt and pepper to taste.

❋ Pour the sauce over the trout and garnish with chopped parsley or chives.

Serves 2

Trout for Breakfast

There is nothing so delicious as a freshly caught trout fried up for breakfast. Here's an Adirondack guide's recipe.

❋ Clean and wash the trout.

❋ Dip it in a little milk.

❋ Dredge it in a mix of cornmeal, flour, and salt and pepper.

❋ Fry it in bacon grease for 6 minutes a side.

❋ Serve it with bacon and Skillet Corn Bread (page 126).

Salmon Mousse

This is great for a lunch or as an appetizer. Use leftover or canned salmon.

I envelope Knox gelatin

1/2 cup hot chicken stock

I cup flaked, cooked salmon

I cup mayonnaise

I teaspoon ketchup

1/2 teaspoon Dijon mustard

3 tablespoons chopped fresh dill

I bunch scallions, sliced thinly,
or I onion, finely chopped

Salt and pepper

Chopped chives, for garnish

❋ In a mixing bowl, soften the gelatin with 1/4 cup cold water. Add the chicken stock and stir until all the gelatin is dissolved. Add the salmon, mayonnaise, ketchup, mustard, dill, and salt and pepper to taste. Stir until well combined.

❋ Pour the mixture into a pretty mold, cover with plastic wrap, and refrigerate overnight or all day.

❋ To unmold the mousse, have a platter ready. Run very hot water in the sink to a depth of 2 inches.

❋ Lower the mold almost to the top edge and count to 10. The hot water melts a little of the gelatin and loosens the mousse, so remove it as soon as you feel it getting loose.

❋ Put the platter on top of the mold and flip it upside-down.

❋ Decorate the platter with the lettuce leaves and sprinkle the chives over the mousse.

Serves 6

Crab Cakes

It's difficult to get fresh crab unless you live on a saltwater bay, so I use canned crab and turkey-stuffing mix.

Two 4-ounce cans crabmeat
(or meat from 2 cooked crabs,
if available)

1 tablespoon Old Bay seasoning

1 cup stuffing mix softened with
2 tablespoons chicken stock

1 egg

1 stalk celery, finely chopped

1 medium onion, chopped

Salt and pepper

2 cups oil for frying
(I use vegetable oil)

❋ Mix all the ingredients, except the oil, together in a bowl. Form the mixture into 8 patties that are 3 inches in diameter.

❋ Put them on a plate and refrigerate for 1 hour. This helps keep them together when you fry them.

❋ In a cast-iron skillet, heat half an inch of oil over medium heat. Add the crab cakes and fry for about 6 minutes a side.

❋ Serve with my cousin Jim's crab cake sauce (recipe below), tartar sauce (page 190), or tartar sauce mixed with ketchup.

Serves 4

Jim's Crab Cake Sauce

1 habañero pepper, chopped

1/2 cup sour cream

2 tablespoons chopped cilantro

1 tablespoon lemon juice

❋ Stir the ingredients together in a small bowl.

Makes about 1 cup

Deep-Fried Fish

I first had this dish after fishing in Lake Champlain all day with a crusty old fisherman. He cleaned the fish and we went to his home to make the batter and fry it up. Use an oily solid fish like bluefish or bass or mackerel.

Oil for frying

1 cup Bisquick

1 cup beer

1 egg

1 tablespoon Old Bay seasoning

Salt and pepper

3 pounds of fish, cleaned and cut into 2-inch pieces

❋ Heat 2 inches of oil in a deep pot (you don't want it to splatter).

❋ In a bowl, stir together the Bisquick, beer, egg, Old Bay seasoning, and salt and pepper. Dip the fish into the batter and coat thoroughly.

❋ Drop 3 or 4 pieces of the battered fish into the oil. Cook for 5 to 6 minutes until golden brown. Drain the cooked fish on a brown paper bag or paper towels.

❋ Repeat with the remaining fish.

❋ Serve with tartar sauce.

Serves 6

Tartar Sauce

1 cup mayonnaise

1 tablespoon Dijon mustard

2 gherkin pickles, chopped

1 tablespoon lemon juice

❋ Mix the ingredients thoroughly in a bowl.

❋ Put a tiny bowl of sauce at each place, or put a dollop on each plate, for dipping.

Serves 6

Jambalaya

This recipe comes from Louisiana and is a Creole rendition of Spanish paella. Paella contains all fish, but jambalaya is a tasty mix of fish, sausage, and ham. In addition to the saffron used in paella, jambalaya uses chili powder.

3 tablespoons butter

1 large onion, finely chopped

1 teaspoon chopped garlic

2 medium red or green bell peppers, cut into strips

1½ teaspoons chili powder

1 cup long-grain white rice

1¼ cups chicken stock

1 cup chopped fresh tomatoes

1/4 teaspoon saffron

1/2 teaspoon dried thyme

1 teaspoon salt

1 teaspoon pepper

2 cups cubed cooked ham, (or ham and turkey mixed)

1 small cooked sausage or sliced kielbasa sausage

12 oysters

12 shrimp, shells removed

Parsley, for garnish

❊ Preheat the oven to 350°F.

❊ In a paella pan, melt the butter over medium heat. Add the onions and brown for 5 minutes.

❊ Add the garlic and the peppers and cook until the peppers soften.

❊ Add the chili powder, then the uncooked rice, and stir for 2 minutes.

❊ Add the chicken stock, tomatoes, saffron, thyme, salt, and pepper. Stir and bring to a boil.

❊ Add the ham and sausage.

❊ Cover and bake for 20 minutes.

❊ Add the shrimp and oysters and bake for 10 minutes more.

❊ Sprinkle parsley over the top to serve.

Serves 6–8

Note: A paella pan is round, large, flat pan with 4-inch sides for stovetop cooking. Use a cast-iron skillet if you don't have a paella pan.

Quick Sauté of Fish Fillet

You may glance in a fish market window and see an array of delicate fillets and wonder, "How do I cook that?" Here's how. White fillets such as sole, snapper, and mahi-mahi are too delicate to grill and they would fall apart. And if you deep-fry them, the flavor is ruined, so sautéing is the solution.

6 fresh fish fillets

Flour for dredging

2 tablespoons butter

1 tablespoon chopped fresh garlic

1 tablespoon chopped fresh thyme

1/2 lemon

Salt and pepper

2 tablespoons chopped fresh parsley leaves

❊ Rinse the fish in very cold water and pat it dry with a cloth or paper towel.

❊ Melt the butter in a cast-iron skillet over medium heat.

❊ Dredge the fillets in a little flour and place in the hot butter (if the butter isn't hot, the fish will stick to the pan). Brown each side for 3 to 5 minutes. Cook the fish in batches if necessary. Transfer the fish to a warm plate.

❊ Add the garlic, thyme, and salt and pepper to taste to the butter in the skillet.

❊ Squeeze the lemon juice into the skillet.

❊ Drizzle the lemon butter over the fish.

❊ Sprinkle fresh chopped parsley on top.

Serves 6

Shrimp Curry

See variation of lamb curry on page 176.

Shrimp Scampi with Orzo

You'll need to let the marinade sit for an hour, and the broth should be hot when you add it, so plan ahead.

I pound fresh shrimp,
peeled and deveined

3 tablespoons virgin olive oil

I tablespoon lemon zest

I teaspoon lemon juice

Salt and pepper

4 cloves of garlic, minced

2 tablespoons unsalted butter

I cup uncooked orzo

1/2 cup white wine

2 cups boiling vegetable broth

Parsley, chopped, for serving.

❊ In a medium-size bowl, mix the shrimp, 1 tablespoon olive oil, the lemon zest, lemon juice, red pepper flakes, salt and pepper, and half the minced garlic. Let it marinate for one hour.

❊ In a large cast-iron fry pan, cook the remaining garlic in the remaining (2 tablespoons) olive oil and the butter until it starts to brown. Add the orzo and ½ teaspoon salt and cook until the orzo looks toasted.

❊ Add the wine and then the boiling-hot vegetable broth, cover the pan and cook at low temperature until the orzo is al dente, about 10 minutes.

❊ Add the shrimp on top of the orzo and cook, covered, until shrimp is pink, about 2 minutes.

❊ Sprinkle parsley on top to serve.

Serves 4

Portuguese Fish Stew

Fish stew differs from town to town all over the Mediterranean, but it always consists of a number of different fish and shellfish cooked together in a tomato and wine sauce. The number and type of fish depends on what's available, and how complex you want to make the dish.

1/2 cup olive oil

3 medium onions

2 cloves garlic

1 medium bunch parsley, chopped

One 12-ounce can tomatoes

3 dozen clams

3 dozen mussels

One 4-ounce can tomato paste

Salt and pepper

2 dozen shrimp with shells off

1/2 box frozen tiny white onions

2 pounds halibut, cut into 2-inch chunks

1 pound bay scallops

3 medium lobsters (optional)

Court bouillon (page 94)

❉ Heat the oil in a large soup pot over medium heat. Add the onions and cook for 10 minutes. Add the garlic, parsley, and tomatoes. Cover and simmer for 30 minutes.

❉ Put the mussels in another large soup pot, and add 1 inch of water. Cover, bring to a boil, and cook for 3 to 5 minutes until the mussels open up.

❉ Transfer the mussels to a bowl and remove all but 6 from their shells (to use for decoration).

❉ Add the clams to the pot and replace the boiled-off liquid. Steam as you did the mussels (keeping 6 clams in their shells).

❉ Reduce the steaming liquid and add 3 tablespoons of it to the tomato mixture for flavor. Save the rest.

❉ Add the lobsters to the pot with 4 cups water and steam for 10 minutes. Discard the cooking water. Cut the tails and claws off and set aside.

❉ Prepare the court bouillon as directed in the recipe.

❉ Boil the shrimp in court bouillon for 5 minutes, then let them cool. Strain the cooking liquid into the tomato mixture.

❉ Add the halibut and scallops to the tomato mixture. Cook for 10 minutes until the halibut is done. Add the shrimp, mussels, and clams. Heat for 4 minutes.

❉ Transfer the stew to a large tureen. Garnish with the 6 mussels and 6 clams in their shells and the lobster pieces.

❉ Serve with French bread.

Serves 8–10

Grandmother's Tea House, later known as the Weekend House, now known as the Huntley Weekend Cottage.

6 Salads & Vegetables

This chapter includes all the important side dishes that complement your main course – salads, vegetables, potatoes, and rice. In the main course chapter, some of these side dishes are recommended for a given meal, but feel free to experiment and prepare what you like according to your taste at the time.

Classic Caesar Salad

My Uncle Sqee (Seymour Ellis) owned four Howard Johnson restaurants during the 1960s. In order to know what the competition was doing, he would eat at everyone else's restaurants. While I was in college in New York, he would invite me along. He was a Caesar salad expert and was not shy about asking to help the waiter do a proper Caesar salad. This is his recipe. For the croutons you can use two slices of any bread – stale or fresh – cut into little cubes. Place on a cookie sheet with 1 tablespoon olive oil and bake for 20 minutes at 350°F.

One 2-ounce can flat anchovies

I cup olive oil

3 tablespoons red wine vinegar

1/2 teaspoon balsamic vinegar

I teaspoon Dijon mustard

Salt and pepper

I head romaine lettuce, soaked
in cold water and cut into
bite-size pieces

I egg yolk (optional)
or I tablespoon heavy cream

1/4 cup grated Parmesan cheese

I cup croutons

❊ Assemble all your ingredients.

❊ Put the anchovies in a large wooden bowl, and mash with a fork. Add the olive oil, vinegar, mustard, salt and pepper to taste, and mix well. Add the egg yolk. (Unless you know it is fresh, use 1 tablespoon heavy cream instead.)

❊ Just before serving, add the cold lettuce and toss. Sprinkle the croutons and the Parmesan on top.

Serves 4

Here's a useful tip for lettuce salads: A friend of mine who runs a catering company outside of Boston showed me his speedy way of preparing lettuce for salad. Cut the stem off, make a slice through the head lengthwise, roll it 90 degrees and slice lengthwise again. Then chop it end to end so that you have bite-size pieces. Soak them in cold water and drain or spin. This is a timesaver especially if you are preparing several heads of lettuce.

Salade Laitue

This is a favorite salad of ours. The recipe is originally from Lyon, France. You may substitute slivered almonds for the hazelnuts if you like, and you may add mandarin orange slices for a variation.

I large head Bibb lettuce

1/2 cup hazelnuts

I teaspoon butter

1/2 cup crumbled Roquefort, Stilton, or other good blue-veined cheese

Mandarin orange slices (optional)

FOR THE DRESSING

1/3 cup extra-virgin olive oil

1/4 cup balsamic vinegar

I teaspoon dried basil

I teaspoon black pepper

Juice from 1/2 lemon

❋ Cut the stem off the bottom of the lettuce, cut the lettuce lengthwise, turn it 90 degrees, cut lengthwise again, then cut in half widthwise. Rinse in very cold water and drain or spin.

❋ Partially crush the hazelnuts with a rolling pin. Grease a pie tin with the butter, add the nuts, and put them under a pre-heated broiler for about 4 minutes or until they turn golden brown. Transfer to a small bowl or plate.

❋ **To make the dressing:** whisk the olive oil, vinegar, basil, pepper, and lemon together in a small measuring cup or jar.

❋ Place the lettuce in a wooden bowl, pour the dressing over it and toss until the leaves are coated. Sprinkle the cheese and nuts on top. Garnish with mandarin orange slices if you like.

Serves 4

Pear Vinaigrette

Here is an alternate dressing for this salad that may be used on fresh field greens as well. It is also good over fresh steamed asparagus that is served cold in the summer.

I cup pear liquid from poaching

I cup olive oil

1/3 cup red vinegar

2 tablespoons balsamic vinegar

I teaspoon sugar

I teaspoon Dijon mustard

❋ Whisk all the ingredients together and apply lightly to the salad or asparagus. This makes enough for 3 to 4 uses, so store the extra in the refrigerator until you need it again.

Makes about 2½ cups

Apple & Walnut Salad

This is a nice wintertime salad.

4 apples, I like Honey Crisp

2 tablespoons apple vinegar, or juice of I lemon

Sea salt and ground pepper to taste

2 tablespoons maple syrup

I cup walnut halves

❋ Core and slice the apples very thinly. Place in large bowl. Drizzle the vinegar (or lemon juice) over the apple slices.

❋ Add sea salt and pepper and stir, flipping the apple slices so all is coated. Add the maple syrup and stir. Taste and adjust seasoning.

❋ Chop walnuts into raisin-size pieces and sprinkle on top of the apples just before serving.

Serves 4

4th of July Salad

Corn in the cob is in season from May (in the South) to September.

6 ears sweet corn on the cob

I bunch of scallions

I jalapeño, seeded and chopped [see CAUTION]

I teaspoon lemon zest

Salt and pepper

4 tablespoons olive oil

2 tablespoons light wine vinegar

I tablespoon fresh lemon juice

1/4 cup chopped parsley

I head of romaine lettuce, chopped up

2 avocados, sliced at the last minute

❋ Cook the corn. Let it cool, then slice off the kernels into a salad bowl. Add the chopped scallions and jalapeño and stir.

❋ Add the lemon zest and salt and pepper and stir. Add the olive oil and vinegar and lemon juice and stir. Add the chopped parsley and the chopped romaine lettuce and toss everything until it looks evenly mixed.

❋ Serve with avocado that has been sliced at the last minute.

CAUTION: Wear gloves, or wash your hands thoroughly with soap after you handle the jalapeño, or if you touch your eyes they will sting!

Serves 4-6

Pineapple Coleslaw

I prefer this sweet coleslaw made with pineapple that I first had at a local pub in Keene, New York, as a teenager.

1/2 head cabbage

8 small carrots, peeled

1 medium sweet onion, chopped

8 ounces canned or fresh pineapple, chopped

2 tablespoons pineapple juice

1/4 cup lemon juice

1 cup mayonnaise

1 teaspoon dried thyme

1/2 teaspoon ground ginger

Salt and pepper

❄ Peel the outside leaves off the cabbage and cut the stem off. Slice the cabbage in half. Chop each piece into small shreds and put in a large salad bowl.

❄ Grate the carrots into the bowl. Add the onion, pineapple, pineapple juice, mayonnaise, thyme, ginger, and salt and pepper to taste. Mix it all up thoroughly.

Note: You can keep coleslaw in a covered glass bowl for 4 or 5 days in the refrigerator. Mayonnaise acts as a preservative but it breaks down in sun or heat. Do not ever leave coleslaw on the picnic table in the sun! Bring it out last and clear it first. If it has been outside for the meal, don't save it.

Serves 8–10

Port & Cherry Molded Salad

This molded salad goes well with red meat. It's slightly sweet and has a nice flavor of port. It's alcoholic unless you boil the port for 1 minute.

2 envelopes Knox gelatin

One 10-ounce can Bing cherries

1 sweet onion, chopped

3 tablespoons fresh herbs;
dill is good

1 cup port (or Marsala
or cream sherry)

Chopped lettuce, for garnish

❄ In a mixing bowl, soften the gelatin with 2 tablespoons cool water.

❄ In a saucepan, heat the cherries and juice. Pour into the mixing bowl and stir to melt the gelatin. Stir in the onion, herbs, and port. Pour the mixture into an 8-inch mold. Cover with plastic wrap and refrigerate for 3 hours.

❄ To unmold, run hot water 6 inches deep in the sink. Lower the mold almost to the top edge and count to 10. Invert the mold onto a platter. Garnish with a bed of chopped lettuce.

Serves 6–8

Tomato Aspic

This was one of my mother's favorites because it is pretty. She loved meals to have a balance of color. For red she would serve beets, sliced tomatoes, or this tomato aspic, which is nice in the summer because it is cool. You can make it several days in advance and keep it refrigerated. Serve it with the dressing below, or use ranch dressing. You will need a pretty 8-inch mold although it is possible to do it in a Pyrex mixing bowl.

2 envelopes Knox gelatin

1/4 cup hot chicken stock

One 15-ounce can V-8 juice

3 stalks celery, finely chopped

1 small onion, finely chopped

1 teaspoon Dijon mustard

3 tablespoons fresh thyme, basil, or dill

Chopped lettuce, for garnish

FOR THE DRESSING

1/2 cup mayonnaise

1/2 cup lemon juice

3 tablespoons cream

❋ In a mixing bowl, soften the gelatin in 2 tablespoons cool water. Stir in the hot chicken stock to melt it. Add the V-8 juice, celery, onion, mustard, and herb. Stir to mix thoroughly.

❋ Pour the mixture into an 8-inch mold.

❋ Cover with plastic wrap and refrigerate until it is solid, about 3 hours.

❋ To unmold the aspic, run very hot water in the sink about 6 inches deep. Lower the mold in almost to the top edge and count to 10. Take the mold out of the water, and invert it onto a platter.

❋ Garnish with a bed of chopped lettuce.

❋ **To make the dressing:** stir together the mayonnaise, lemon juice, and cream in a small bowl.

Serves 8

Sweet and Sour Orzo Salad

Easy and refreshing.

FOR THE SALAD

3/4 cups orzo

1 cup chopped cucumber
(1 medium cucumber)

1 red pepper, chopped

1 apple, chopped

8 cherry tomatoes, cut in half

1/2 cup chopped chives or
chopped scallions

FOR THE DRESSING

½ cup olive oil

1 lemon, squeezed

1/4 teaspoon red pepper

1 teaspoon dried dill

1 tablespoon fresh dill, chopped

1 tablespoon sugar

Salt and pepper

❋ Cook the orzo according to the directions on the package. You should have 1½ cups for the recipe.

❋ Toss the orzo with the other ingredients.

To make the dressing: Whisk it all together and pour over the salad.

Serves 4

Corn Pudding

Delicious with grilled or roasted meat, this dish is even good for breakfast! You can use fresh, frozen, or canned corn.

3 pieces soft white bread
(you want this to disappear as it
cooks so don't use French bread
or any other dense bread)

2 cups corn kernels

I red bell pepper, chopped

I medium onion, chopped

3 eggs

I ½ cups half-and-half

1/4 teaspoon nutmeg

Salt and pepper

❋ Preheat the oven to 350°F. Grease an ovenproof baking dish.

❋ Line the prepared dish with the bread. Distribute the corn evenly over the bread. Sprinkle the red pepper and onion over the corn.

❋ In a separate bowl, beat together the eggs, half-and-half, nutmeg, and salt and pepper to taste. Pour this mixture into the baking dish.

❋ Bake for 35 to 40 minutes, until the pudding is firm in the middle. The texture of the cooked pudding should be like scrambled eggs. Cooking time will depend on the pan you use.

If you bake this in a bowl, it will take longer than in a large flat pan.

Serves 8

Spinach Casserole

This is really a form of creamed spinach cooked in the oven. It's a great dish when you are serving lots of people.

4 ounces cream cheese

4 ounces cottage cheese

1/2 pint sour cream

2 cups heavy cream

4 eggs

1/4 teaspoon nutmeg

Salt and pepper

4 bags fresh spinach or four 10-ounce boxes frozen whole leaf spinach

2 tablespoons butter

8 cloves garlic, chopped

1 medium onion, chopped

❋ Preheat the oven to 350°F.

❋ Have all the ingredients at room temperature. In a mixing bowl, mix the cream cheese, cottage cheese, sour cream, heavy cream, eggs, nutmeg, and salt and pepper together.

❋ Sauté the fresh spinach in butter with the garlic until it is wilted (thaw frozen spinach first then sauté it quickly).

❋ Place the spinach in an ovenproof dish. Sprinkle the onions over it. Pour the cream and egg mixture on top.

❋ Bake for 40 minutes, until it has puffed up and browned a little on top. A knife will come out clean when it is done.

Serves 8

Creamed Spinach

Spinach is loaded with iron, antioxidants, and vitamins, so we probably could live on it.

1 tablespoon butter

1/2 sweet onion, chopped (Maui, Vidalia, red onion, or scallions)

One 8-ounce bag spinach, washed

1/2 cup heavy cream mixed with 1/4 cup sour cream

1/4 teaspoon nutmeg

Salt and pepper

❋ In a frying pan, heat the butter over medium heat. Add the onion and sauté until it is translucent. Add the spinach, cover, and cook for 5 minutes over low heat until it is wilted. Transfer the spinach to a board and chop it. Boil off the liquid in the pan and return the spinach to the pan.

❋ Stir in the heavy cream-sour cream mixture. Add the nutmeg and salt and pepper to taste. Cook until the cream thickens – about 4 to 5 minutes.

Serves 4

Veggie Stacks

This is an easy recipe but it looks complicated. Each guest will be served a colorful stack of summer vegetables.

2 tablespoons regular olive oil

1 eggplant, peeled and cut into 1/2-inch-thick rounds

2 yellow squash, peeled and cut into 1/2-inch-thick rounds

2 zucchini, peeled and cut into 1/2-inch-thick rounds

2 red bell peppers, cut into 1-inch-square pieces

2 onions, halved and cut into thin slices

1 basket cherry tomatoes

8 ounces goat cheese

2 tablespoons virgin olive oil

2 tablespoons chopped fresh dill

❋ Preheat the broiler.

❋ Oil a large baking sheet with the olive oil. Place all of the veggies on it.

❋ Broil the veggies for 7 minutes, turning them once.

❋ Take them out of the oven. Let the veggies cool a bit.

❋ To assemble, start with the eggplant, top with a slice of goat cheese (you will spread a little cheese between each vegetable layer) then the yellow squash, zucchini, red pepper, onion, and top with a cherry tomato.

❋ Repeat to make 8 stacks.

❋ Drizzle a little of the olive oil on each stack and top with some of the dill.

❋ Serve at room temperature. If they are too hot, the cheese will ooze out.

Serves 8

Ratatouille

This is a terrific vegetable stew and a favorite French dish for the end of summer when the garden suddenly has too many eggplant, squash, and tomatoes ripe at once – voila, a stew. This is a great dish on a cool fall or cold winter night as well.

2 tablespoons olive oil

6 tomatoes, cut into 2-inch chunks

2 zucchini, cut into 2-inch chunks

1 eggplant, cut into 2-inch chunks

2 onions, cut into 2-inch chunks

2 green onions, cut into 2-inch chunks

One 8-ounce can whole Italian tomatoes

1 tablespoon chopped basil leaves

1 tablespoon chopped oregano leaves

1 tablespoon chopped thyme leaves

Salt and pepper

❋ Heat the olive oil in a heavy pot over low heat. Add the remaining ingredients and cook for 1 hour, stirring occasionally.

Serves 8–10

Variation: Put leftover ratatouille into an ovenproof dish and sprinkle a mixture of Parmesan and mozzarella cheeses on top. Bake at 350°F for 20 minutes.

Roasted Vegetables

The more colorful your service platter, the better this will look. Buy what is ripe and available regardless of the following list, but always include sweet onions and make sure you have lots of different-colored vegetables. Figure one vegetable per person so if you use the following list this recipe will serve about 12. We prepare this dish often when we have large parties because it can be prepared in advance and served at room temperature. Of course, you can cook them up right before dinner and serve them hot. The recipe calls for broiling but you can grill the vegetables if you like.

1 bunch asparagus, bottom third of stems removed

1 box cherry tomatoes

2 medium sweet onions

1 eggplant

2 zucchini

2 yellow squash

2 red, orange, or yellow bell peppers

2 green bell peppers

2 tablespoons regular olive oil

2 tablespoons fresh chopped basil (or 2 teaspoons dried)

2 tablespoons virgin olive oil

1 tablespoon garlic powder

❋ Preheat the broiler.

❋ Wash and cut the vegetables into bite-size pieces (except the asparagus and tomatoes).

❋ Oil a large cookie sheet with the regular olive oil and put the veggies on it.

❋ Sprinkle the basil over the veggies.

❋ Broil for about 8 minutes, or until the edges of the vegetables turn dark brown, turning them once.

❋ Transfer the vegetables to a serving platter. Drizzle with the virgin olive oil and sprinkle with the garlic powder.

Serves 10–12

Winter Squash & Mushroom Curry

Turmeric is good for your immune system.

3 tablespoons olive oil

I medium/large butternut squash, peeled, seeded, and cut into cubes

I jalapeño [see CAUTION]

2 garlic cloves, minced

3 shallots, diced

I teaspoon Dijon mustard

I teaspoon curry powder

1/2 teaspoon cumin

I teaspoon coriander

1/2 teaspoon turmeric

Pinch of cayenne pepper

Salt and pepper

I pound mushrooms of various types, cleaned and sliced

I cup coconut milk

2 tablespoons lime juice

Cilantro for garnish

❊ In a large cast-iron fry pan, sauté the squash cubes in the olive oil on medium high until they start to brown.

❊ Remove from the pan to a plate.

❊ Put into the fry pan: the jalapeño with a slit down one side (it will be removed after cooking), the shallots, the garlic, mustard, curry, cumin, coriander, turmeric, cayenne pepper, salt and pepper.

❊ Add the shallots, stir to coat them with spices, and cook until they are clear.

❊ Add the squash back into the fry pan.

❊ Add the mushrooms and sauté until they are cooked. Do not cover the pan or the mushrooms will become rubbery.

❊ Remove the jalapeño and discard it.

❊ Add the coconut milk and stir.

❊ Add the lime juice and stir.

❊ Serve with cilantro sprinkled on top.

CAUTION: When handling the jalapeño, wear tight-fitting hospital gloves, or wash your hands thoroughly with soap afterwards. Otherwise, if you touch your eyes they will sting!

Serves 6

7 Desserts

Dessert is usually the first thing I cook to get it out of the way, which is why most of these recipes can be made in advance. Tiramisu should be prepared a day before serving. Puddings can be done early and reheated. Pies can be done in the morning and left at room temperature. Of course, the soufflé must be done at the last minute, so be sure to prepare a simple meal before serving this spectacular dessert.

Note: The recipes for the first six desserts listed here can be found in Chapter 1 with the dinner menus.

Pumpkin Bread Pudding with Raspberry Sauce

Everyone says "What is this? It's so good." The pumpkin gives the pudding a tangy taste and it's a great way to use those Halloween pumpkins. Cut them in half and scoop out the seeds. Bake them upside down in a pan with ½ inch of water for 40 minutes at 350°F. Cool, and then scoop out the "meat." Freeze what you don't use today in freezer bags.

FOR THE PUDDING

3 cups stale bread (French, white, sourdough, or whole wheat)

1 cup cooked or canned pumpkin

1 ½ cups milk

1/2 cup heavy cream

3 eggs

1/2 cup sugar

2 teaspoons cinnamon

1/4 teaspoon nutmeg

1 teaspoon vanilla extract

1/2 teaspoon ground ginger

FOR THE SAUCE

1 cup raspberries

1/2 cup sugar

1 tablespoon lemon juice

1/4 teaspoon cinnamon

❄ Preheat the oven to 350°F.

❄ **To make the pudding:** Place the bread in a lasagna-type baking dish.

❄ In a bowl, mix the remaining pudding ingredients together with a fork. Pour this mixture over the bread and let it soak in for 15 minutes before baking.

❄ Bake for 45 minutes or until a knife goes in and comes out clean.

❄ **To make the sauce:** Combine the sauce ingredients in a small saucepan. Bring to a boil and simmer for 10 minutes until the berries are just breaking up. (If you boil it too much, you will have the very best raspberry jam!)

❄ Remove the pan from the heat and immediately transfer the sauce to a serving dish. Or if you want a smooth sauce, puree it in a blender or food processor first.

❄ Serve the pudding warm with the raspberry sauce or heavy cream.

Serves 6

Rice Pudding

Here's a good way to use leftover rice, and it's so easy. White rice, long grain white, and jasmine rice all work well.

3 eggs

2 cups half-and-half

1/3 cup sugar

I teaspoon cinnamon

1/4 teaspoon nutmeg

I teaspoon vanilla extract

2 cups cooked white rice

1/2 cup raisins

❄ Preheat the oven to 350°F.

❄ In a bowl beat the eggs with the half-and-half. Beat in the sugar, spices, and vanilla. Stir in the rice, then the raisins. Pour the mixture into a baking dish.

❄ Bake for 30 to 40 minutes, until it is firm in the center when you jiggle it.

Serves 6–8

Indian Pudding

I first had this old-fashioned dessert in Boston when I was in college. You can still find it there, but almost nowhere else. This dense, sweet, and spicy pudding probably kept the Puritans alive.

3 cups milk

1/2 cup cornmeal

I cup water

2 eggs, beaten

1/2 cup sugar

1/2 cup molasses

I teaspoon cinnamon

1/2 teaspoon ground ginger

1/4 teaspoon salt

I cup raisins

❄ Preheat the oven to 300°F.

❄ In a saucepan, bring 2 cups of the milk to a boil. Lower the heat and whisk in the cornmeal. Stir in the remaining ingredients. Pour the mixture into an ovenproof dish and pour the remaining 1 cup of milk on top.

❄ Bake for 1 hour.

❄ Serve hot with vanilla ice cream.

Serves 6–8

Pears Belle Hélène

These are poached pears served with a custard sauce. Any brown spots disappear, so it is a nice way to use pears that are tasty but look less than perfect. You can poach the pears whole or cut them in half – it depends on what you serve for dinner or how hungry your guests are; we prefer the pears halved.

FOR THE PEARS

4 fresh, almost-ripe pears (they need a little hardness to withstand the poaching intact)

1/2 cup sugar mixed with 1 cup water

Zest of 1/2 lemon

FOR THE CUSTARD SAUCE

2 eggs

2 cups half-and-half

1/2 cup sugar

1 teaspoon cinnamon

1/4 teaspoon nutmeg

1 teaspoon vanilla extract

❄ **To poach the pears:** Cut the pears in half (or leave whole if preferred) and peel them. Remove the center section with seeds. Place them cut side down in a saucepan with the sugar water and lemon zest. Bring to a boil and simmer for 20 minutes.

❄ Transfer the pears to a pretty serving dish or individual bowls.

❄ **To make the sauce:** In a saucepan, whisk the eggs and half-and-half over medium heat. Once the custard starts to thicken, stir it with a wooden spoon. When it coats the spoon (about 7 minutes, it should stick to the spoon like thick gravy) remove the pan from the heat.

❄ Pour the sauce over the pears. Refrigerate if you don't want to serve the pears warm.

Serves 4, using whole pears; 8, if using pear halves

Note: If you like, you can reduce the poaching liquid to 1 cup and use it for the **Pear Vinaigrette** on page 199.

Floating Island

My mother served this in the 1950s. It is a pretty dish served in a flat glass bowl with little meringues floating on custard. I have seen it served recently in fancy New York City restaurants, so it seems (like many things mid-century) to be making a comeback!

FOR THE SAUCE

1 recipe Custard Sauce (page 214)

FOR THE MERINGUES

4 egg whites

1 teaspoon cream of tartar

3 tablespoons sugar

Zest of 1/2 lemon, grated

❊ Prepare the custard sauce as directed in the recipe. Pour the custard into 6 individual serving bowls or a large wide bowl with low sides to accommodate the floating islands of meringue.

❊ **To make the meringues:** Using a mixer, beat the egg whites with the cream of tartar until they are very stiff. Stir in the sugar.

❊ Use a wide, low-sided pan (like a sauté pan) so you can poach 3 or 4 meringues at a time. Bring 2 inches of water to a slow boil – the water should barely move. Add the lemon zest.

❊ With a large spoon, drop 3 or 4 spoonfuls of the egg white mixture into the boiling water; do not crowd them. Simmer for 3 minutes or until firm.

❊ Using a slotted spoon, transfer the meringues to the bowl(s) with the custard.

❊ Repeat the process until you have cooked 12 meringues.

Serves 6

Grand Marnier Soufflé

This is not exactly camp cooking but it is a great soufflé. Since it only cooks for 15 minutes, give your guests a light salad, more wine, and a tasty cheese course while they wait for this special dessert. Go to the kitchen to beat the egg whites – your guests won't mind the wait when this comes out! Note that you will need a cold wet cloth or a bed of ice ready before you start this recipe. A metal soufflé dish will conduct the heat better, but any deep, straight-sided, ovenproof dish will work.

5 egg yolks

1/3 cup plus 3 tablespoons sugar

1/3 cup Grand Marnier

1 tablespoon grated orange zest

7 egg whites

1/4 teaspoon cream of tartar

❈ Preheat the oven to 425°F.

❈ Butter the soufflé dish and tap 3 tablespoons of the sugar around the sides until the entire inside is coated with butter and sugar. Discard the excess sugar.

❈ Beat the yolks and the 1/3 cup sugar in a saucepan over low heat until it thickens and turns light yellow.

❈ Stir in the Grand Marnier and the orange zest.

❈ Set the saucepan on a cold wet cloth or on a bed of ice to stop the cooking. You can do this step ahead.

❈ Use a mixer to beat the egg whites with the cream of tartar until they are very stiff.

❈ Use a rubber spatula to mix a little egg white into the yolk mixture.

❈ Pour the yolk mixture into the egg whites and carefully fold the whites in without losing the air. Don't be fussy here – it's OK to have blobs of yolk and white unmixed.

❈ Pour this mixture into the soufflé pan.

❈ Bake for 15 minutes or until puffed and browned. Serve immediately.

As the soufflé cools, it will fall.

Serves 6

Pecan Pie

My first mother-in-law, a real Southern lady, taught me this recipe. It is an authentic Southern pecan pie.

One 8-inch piecrust

3/4 cup pecan halves

3 eggs

I cup sugar

1/2 cup dark Karo syrup

I teaspoon flour

3 tablespoons melted butter

Whipped cream for serving

❄ Preheat the oven to 275°F.

❄ Place the piecrust in an 8-inch pie plate. Line the piecrust with the pecans.

❄ In a bowl beat the eggs.

❄ Add the sugar, Karo syrup, flour, and melted butter and mix until smooth.

❄ Pour this mixture into the pie dish. The pecans will float to the top.

❄ Bake for $1\frac{1}{2}$ hours or until it barely jiggles in the center when you move it. The center will harden as it cools.

❄ Serve with whipped cream

Serves 6–8

Apple Pie

Here is the all-American classic dessert, but with raisins.

4 medium size apples, sliced thin

1/2 cup sugar

1 tablespoon flour

Juice of 1/2 lemon

1/2 teaspoon cinnamon

1/4 teaspoon nutmeg

1/4 cup chopped walnuts or pecans

1/4 cup raisins

Two 10-inch piecrusts

❋ Preheat the oven to 350°F.

❋ In a bowl, combine all the ingredients except the piecrusts.

❋ Place one of the piecrusts in a 10-inch pie plate. Transfer the apple mixture to the pie plate. Dot with butter and place the other piecrust on top.

❋ Crimp the crusts together using your fingers. Make 3 little slashes in the top crust to let out steam as the apples cook.

❋ Bake for 40 minutes or until the crust is brown. Cool before serving.

Serves 6–8

The Uplands kitchen

Pot de Crème or Crème Brûlée

Can you tell that I love dairy products? My grandfather was a gentleman farmer in the summers. The rest of the year he was a lawyer in New York City, but if you asked what he did, he would say "I'm a farmer." And so he was – he owned the Uplands Meadow Dairy that supplied most of the milk, eggs, cheese, and cream to the Keene Valley and Keene area in the 1920s, '30s, and '40s. As a result, we had lots of very fresh dairy products, and I learned to love them.

The same custard is used for both pot de crème and crème brûlée. The pot de crème is simply served after it thickens on top of the stove. For crème brûlée, the custard is put into an ovenproof dish, covered with sugar, and broiled or flamed until the sugar melts into a golden caramelized crust.

4 egg yolks

5 tablespoons sugar

2 cups heavy cream

1/8 teaspoon salt

1 tablespoon grated lemon
or orange zest

2 tablespoons Grand Marnier
(or any fruit liqueur)

❋ In a bowl, beat the egg yolks and sugar together to a thick, light yellow color.

❋ In a saucepan, heat the cream over medium heat almost to the boiling point.

❋ Beat the cream into the egg yolk mixture, then pour it into the saucepan.

❋ Add the salt, zest, and liqueur and cook until it is thick enough to coat a wooden spoon, about 10 minutes.

❋ Pour the custard into little pots or dishes. Refrigerate if serving more than 3 hours later.

❋ To make **crème brûlée**, sprinkle a teaspoon of sugar on top of each pot and flame the sugar with a butane match torch (or under broiler) until it gets brown.

❋ For the **pots de crème**, shave some chocolate on top.

Variation: For **chocolate pot de crème**, add 4 ounces of sweetened chocolate to the cream as you are heating it (break it into small pieces and stir until it is all melted with the almost boiling cream).

Serves 8

Walnut Roll

This is a vanilla soufflé with ground walnuts cooked in a jelly roll pan then rolled up with flavored whipped cream. With its light and airy slices and sweet filling this is an absolutely divine dessert.

Note: A jelly roll pan is 10 by 20 inches with half-inch sides.

FOR THE SOUFFLÉ

6 eggs, separated

3/4 cup sugar

1 teaspoon baking powder

1 cup walnuts or pecans, ground up

FOR THE FILLING

1 ½ cups whipped cream

2 tablespoons confectioners' sugar

1 tablespoon instant coffee or cocoa or both

1/2 cup confectioners' sugar

❄ Preheat the oven to 375°F.

❄ **To make the soufflé:** Butter a jelly roll pan and line it with 3 big pieces of wax paper one on top of the other and overlapping the ends. Butter the wax paper.

❄ Using a mixer, beat the egg yolks with the sugar until they are thick and light yellow. Stir in the baking powder and nuts.

❄ In another bowl, use the mixer to beat the egg whites until stiff.

❄ Fold the yolk mixture into the whites carefully so the whites don't lose the air.

❄ Pour this into the jelly roll pan, smoothing to the edges.

❄ Bake for 15 minutes. (It will look puffy in some places and lumpy in others.)

❄ Cover the pan with 3 pieces of wax paper and a damp kitchen towel. Let the soufflé cool for 15 minutes.

❄ **To make the filling:** In a bowl, stir the filling ingredients together gently to combine. Set aside.

❄ Remove the towel from the soufflé and flip the jelly roll pan upside down on the counter so the 3 pieces of wax paper are on the bottom and the 3 lining the pan are on the top.

❄ Remove the wax paper from the top (some of the soufflé will stick to the paper).

❄ Cut about 1/2 inch off the edges of the roll all around. Don't leave them on or the roll will not roll smoothly.

❄ Spread the filling around but not to the very edge.

❄ Taking the long side of roll with the 3 pieces of wax paper roll up 1/3 of the roll. Fold the wax paper back and using it as leverage, flip the last third of the roll over. Cut the wax paper off leaving the slim piece still under the roll. Using this slim piece of wax paper, slide the roll onto a long thin platter.

❄ Keep cool until serving.

❄ Just before serving, sprinkle confectioners' sugar over the top.

Serves 8–10

Chocolate Chip Cookies with Nuts

You can put the dough in a resealable plastic bag and freeze or refrigerate it if you only want to make a few cookies at a time. My husband, Neil, and I often have fruit for dessert with these cookies. We bake only two dozen (rather than the standard four dozen) so they're hot and fresh. Of course these are good to take on hikes.

2 sticks butter, softened

1 ¼ cups brown sugar

1/2 cup granulated sugar

2 eggs

1 teaspoon vanilla extract

2 cups flour

1 teaspoon baking soda

1 teaspoon salt

1 ½ cups chocolate chips

1 cup chopped walnuts, pecans, or macadamia nuts

❄ Preheat the oven to 350°F.

❄ Cream the butter and sugars together (using the single arm of the mixer, or a big wooden spoon and the mixing bowl).

❄ Mix in the eggs and vanilla.

❄ Add the flour, baking soda, and salt, and mix well.

❄ Stir in the chocolate chips and nuts.

❄ Drop the dough by tablespoons onto cookie sheets, leaving 2 inches in between cookies.

❄ Bake for 15 minutes.

❄ Using a spatula, transfer the cookies to a board or tin foil on the counter to cool. Do not let them cool on the cookie sheet or they will stick and fall apart as you try to remove them.

Makes 2 dozen small cookies

Jams & Jellies

When I visited my friend Rosaline Crowley in Madison, Connecticut one early July day, I smelled wonderful strawberry and cinnamon aromas. She had picked a large basket of strawberries and was making jam in a huge washtub on the stove. She convinced me that it was not difficult. Her rules: Use as much sugar as fruit; use lemon or lime juice to thicken the fruit; and use cinnamon and nutmeg for flavor.

For jams and jellies you need hot, sterilized jars. When you put hot jam into a hot jar and put sterilized lids on top, it creates a vacuum seal as it cools. Save all those jam jars so that you have them when you need them. Don't think of the sugar that you are eating – focus on the Vitamin C!

Strawberry Jam

This is my rendition of Rosaline's recipe. Her jam is better than mine because she picks the berries when they are ripe and sweet, while I tend to buy them at the store. If you have the opportunity to go to a strawberry farm and pick your own berries, it is worth the trip for superior jam. Store berries are picked before they are completely ripe so that they will travel well.

4 cups washed strawberries, sliced

4 cups sugar

Juice of 1 lemon

1 tablespoon cinnamon

1/4 teaspoon nutmeg

Six 8-ounce vacuum-seal jelly jars

❋ Place the strawberries in a large saucepan (when the jam boils the first time, it will rise up the sides, so choose a LARGE pan). Add the sugar, lemon juice, and spices. Bring to a boil and boil for 1 minute, stirring occasionally.

❋ Lower the heat to a simmer and cook for 1 hour.

❋ While the jam is cooking, boil the jars and lids for at least 5 minutes.

❋ The jam will thicken and glisten when it is done. With a large spoon, skim the foam off the top. Ladle the jam into the hot jars. Wipe the edge of the jar with a wet cloth; any drip of jam on the jar edge will ruin the vacuum seal. Put the lid on tight.

Makes 6 jars

Peach Jam

Follow the strawberry jam recipe above, substituting peaches for the strawberries.

Marmalade

A houseguest gave me a jar of her marmalade, which was divine. "How do you make it?" I asked at break-fast. "Oh, it is so easy" she said, and told me the following recipe, which I wrote down as she drove away.

4 navel oranges, cut in half

I grapefruit, cut in half

I lemon, cut in half

5 pound bag of sugar

I tablespoon cinnamon

1/4 teaspoon nutmeg

1/4 teaspoon ground ginger

1/4 teaspoon ground cloves

Six to eight 8-ounce vacuum seal jelly jars

❄ Squeeze the fruit over a very large heavy pot to extract some juice, then put the fruit in the pot. Cover and cook over medium heat for 30 minutes.

❄ Transfer the fruit to a strainer placed over a bowl to catch the juices. Let the fruit cool or use rubber gloves. Place the fruit on a board and slice the skins very thin. Return the fruit and juices to the pot. Stir in the sugar and spices. Bring to a boil, stirring occasionally. Lower the heat to a simmer for 1 hour.

❄ During the hour, boil the jars and lids for at least 5 minutes.

❄ Ladle the marmalade into the hot jars. Wipe the edge of the jar with a wet cloth; any drip of jam on the jar edge will ruin the vacuum seal. Put the lid on tight.

Makes about 8 jars

The Uplands breezeway

Grape Jelly

We planted three Concord grape vines in the garden. About three years went by without any grapes. Then one day I noticed the dogs eating off of the vines and found they were heavy with ripe purple grapes hidden under the leaves. This recipe is the result. This is made just like jam, but by straining out the seeds and skin, it becomes jelly.

2 pounds Concord grapes

2 pounds sugar

1 tablespoon cinnamon

1/2 teaspoon nutmeg

Zest and juice of 1 lemon

Six 8-ounce vacuum-seal jelly jars

❊ Put all the ingredients in a large pot and bring to a boil, stirring occasionally. Lower the heat and simmer for 1 hour, or until the jam has thickened and looks shiny.

❊ During the hour, boil 6–8 jars and lids for at least 5 minutes.

❊ Strain the mixture into another large pot, pressing down on the pulp in the strainer with a wooden spoon. Discard the seeds and pulp in the strainer.

❊ Reheat the jelly for 5 minutes, then ladle the hot jelly into hot jars. Wipe the edge of the jar with a wet cloth; any drip of jelly will ruin the vacuum seal. Put the lid on tight.

Makes 6 jars

Peach Chutney

I had a bowl of peaches ripening for breakfast when I noticed that they would probably begin rotting by morning – so I made this chutney instead. It goes well with all grilled meats.

6 ripe peaches

3 cups sugar

1 onion, chopped

1 cup raisins

1/2 cup balsamic vinegar

❊ Chop the peaches into thumbnail-size chunks. Put all the ingredients into a pot.

❊ Bring to a boil and boil for 1 minute, stirring occasionally. Lower the heat and simmer for 30 minutes. Let the chutney cool before transferring it to a pretty serving bowl.

❊ Store it in the refrigerator in a large jar. It will keep for 3 weeks.

Makes one 12-ounce jar

Index of Recipes

(list of memoir essays is on page 8)